Genealogical Abstracts of the Cumberland Presbyterian Church

Volume One
1836 and Beyond

Sherida K. Eddlemon

HERITAGE BOOKS
2019

HERITAGE BOOKS
AN IMPRINT OF HERITAGE BOOKS, INC.

Books, CDs, and more—Worldwide

For our listing of thousands of titles see our website
at
www.HeritageBooks.com

Published 2019 by
HERITAGE BOOKS, INC.
Publishing Division
5810 Ruatan Street
Berwyn Heights, Md. 20740

Copyright © 1995 Sherida K. Eddlemon

All rights reserved. No part of this book may be reproduced or transmitted in any form or by any means, electronic or mechanical, including photocopying, recording or by any information storage and retrieval system without written permission from the author, except for the inclusion of brief quotations in a review.

International Standard Book Numbers
Paperbound: 978-0-7884-0255-5
Clothbound: 978-0-7884-7515-3

ACKNOWLEDGEMENTS

I want to thank Susan Gore, Director, Historical Foundation of the Cumberland Presbyterian Church, for her support. The information used in preparing the Preface of this work was taken from the information handouts courtesy of the Historical Foundation of the Cumberland Presbyterian Church.

TABLE OF CONTENTS

ARKANSAS

Prairie Grove C. P. Church 19
    Prairie Grove, Washington County

Rock Springs - Oak Grove C. P. Church 92
    Hector, Pope County

ILLINOIS

Shiloh - Mount Pleasant C. P. Church 60
    Virginia, Cass County

KENTUCKY

Sand Springs - Mount Pleasant C. P. Church 36
    Utica, Daviess County

Shady Grove C. P. Church 82
    Wingo, Graves County

MISSISSIPPI

Hernando C. P. Church 35
    Hernando, DeSoto County

MISSOURI

Shawnee Mound C. P. Church 1
    Chilhowee, Johnson County

Huntsville C. P. Church 17
    Huntsville, Randolph County

MISSOURI CONTINUED

Ely - Union Valley C. P. Church 23
    Ely, Marion County

Mount Hope C. P. Church 31
    Huntsville, Randolph County

Rochester C. P. Church 87
    Helena, Andrew County

Surprise C. P. Church 65
    Clinton, Lafayette County

Watson C. P. Church 49
    Watson, Atchison County

Keysville C. P. Church 79
    Crooked Creek, Crawford County

Union Chapel C. P. Church 100
    Jacksonville, Randolph County

TENNESSEE

Cave Spring C. P. Church 13
    Cave Spring, Overton County

Parkes Station - Zion C. P. Church 40
    Parkes Station, Maury County

Alred - Shiloh C. P. Church 42
    Alred, Overton County

Post Oak - Spence's Chapel C. P. Church 84
    Sugar Tree, Decatur County

Beaver Creek C. P. Church 90
    Beaver Creek, Knox County

Granville C. P. Church 69
    Granville, Jackson County

Silver Creek C. P. Church 98
    Silver Creek, Maury County

PREFACE

In Philadelphia, Pennsylvania in 1706 the first Presbytery of the Presbyterian Church of America was organized. As pioneers moved westward into Kentucky and Tennessee an additional presbytery was created in 1802 to encompass this region. This new presbytery was named the "Cumberland Presbytery" after the "Cumberland Region" it covered.

The Cumberland region included Kentucky, Tennessee and parts of Virginia. The area became known as "Cumberland Country" since the pioneers had to cross over the Cumberland Mountains and through the Cumberland Gap to reach the territory. The Cumberland Mountains, Gap and even the Cumberland River that flows through this area derived their name from the British Duke of Cumberland, William Augustus, the third son of George the II. In 1746 as Commander of the English Army he won an important victory at Collodden. The American Colonies honored him by naming the westward Mountains and one of the areas principal rivers after him.

In 1796 in Logan County, Kentucky, a "revival" had broken out and was supported by the majority of the ministers and licentiates of the Cumberland Presbytery. The revival rejected the double unconditional predestination of the Westminster Confession of Faith. This rejected Westminster Confession of Faith stated that God unconditionally chose some persons for salvation and the rest to damnation. The struggling pioneers opposed this doctrine. They believed that no one goes to hell who does not have a chance to go to heaven. They believed in atonement and that it was possible for everyone to be saved. They made no claim as being the only true church and supported many other denominations. The other denominations were regarded as different ways the invisible church expresses its beliefs. The "invisible" church included the true believers of all churches including those persons not belonging to any organized church, that believed in God and Christ. The Kentucky Synod appointed a Commission in 1805 to review the situation. The Commission prohibited a number of ministers and licentiates from administering the Sacraments and preaching the gospel. This created a huge upheaval and these "prohibited" ministers and their supporters and sympathizers organized their own Council and continued to preach the gospel.

The Cumberland Presbytery was dissolved in 1806 by the Kentucky Synod and transferred some of its ministers into other areas.

The newly created Council was unable to reconcile with the Presbyterian Church. On February 4, 1810 in Dickson, Tennessee, at his home Samuel McAdow and two other ministers, Finis Ewing and Samuel King established an independent Presbytery and named it the "Cumberland Presbytery." There was still hopes of a reconciliation, but it never came to pass. Finally in 1813 the "Cumberland Presbytery" had grown so huge it was decided to create a "Cumberland Synod" and divide the area into three smaller presbyteries. The members of the "Cumberland Synod" called themselves "Cumberland Presbyterian" to distinguish them from other Presbyterians.

The new denomination that was created was called the "Cumberland Presbyterian Church." The Cumberland Synod continued until 1829 when the General Assembly was organized in Princeton, Kentucky.

The Cumberland Presbyterian Church today still recognizes all churches that acknowledge Jesus Christ as Savior and Lord. The Confession of faith was revised in 1883 and for a third time in 1984 to keep pace with our contemporary times.

The originals of the records included in this volume are held at the Historical Foundation of the Cumberland Presbyterian Church, Memphis, Tennessee. The Historical Foundation will not do any genealogical research. They are not equipped to reply to written correspondence. The records are not indexed and unless you know the name of the church your ancestor was a member of, it is almost impossible to locate anything. Individuals coming in person to research the records must have an appointment as space is very limited.

Only information of genealogical interest has been abstracted from the church record books. In many of the churches a surname in parentheses appears after the names of women. In most cases, it is their newly married name or in a few instances the maiden name of a married woman. It is not indicated on any records whether it is the married or maiden name. These surnames in the parentheses are included in the index.

The following abbreviations have been used in this volume:

d.	-	died	MG	-	Minister
BD	-	Baptism Date	BAPT	-	Baptism
MD	-	Marriage Date	PRTS	-	Parents
DIS	-	Dismissed	SUS	-	Suspended
EXP	-	Expelled	AD/ADM	-	Admission
PP/p	-	Pages/Page	b.	-	born

These early church records are a previously untapped rich resource for the genealogical researchers. In many cases it is only in these records that the marriage, birth and death dates of an elusive ancestor is recorded. Good luck in your search and hopefully you will find your ancestor within these pages.

Shawnee Mound Cumberland Presbyterian Church, Chilhowee,
Johnson County, Missouri

Register of Adult Baptisms

Name	Date	Reverend
Mary Moore	Aug. 20, 1869	B. F. Thomas
Mary Jane Guian	Aug. 20, 1869	B. F. Thomas
Peter Smiley	Aug. 20, 1869	B. F. Thomas
Ferdinand W. Crooks	Aug. 23, 1869	B. F. Thomas
Ellen Thresher	Aug. 23, 1869	B. F. Thomas
William P. Moore	Nov. 19, 1869	B. F. Thomas
Daniel Grey	Nov. 19, 1869	B. F. Thomas
Margaret Jane Wade	May 22, 1870	B. F. Thomas
Margaret Gowens	Aug. 21, 1870	B. F. Thomas
Martha J. Hays	Aug. 22, 1870	B. F. Thomas
Julie F. Glasgow	Aug. 22, 1870	B F. Thomas
Joseph Mays	Aug. 22, 1870	B. F. Thomas
Martha Grey	Aug. 22, 1870	B. F. Thomas
Carry Powers	Aug. 18, 1870	B. F. Thomas
Jacob Wiseman	Aug. 22, 1870	B. F. Thomas
Anna Wiseman	Aug. 22, 1870	B. F. Thomas
Andrew Russell	Aug. 22, 1870	B. F. Thomas
Amanda Cassy	Aug. 22, 1870	B. F. Thomas
Robert B. Smith	Aug. 22, 1870	B. F. Thomas
Margarett E. Smith	Aug. 22, 1870	B. F. Thomas
Susan J. Crabtree	Aug. 22, 1870	B. F. Thomas
Susan Kimsey	Aug. 22, 1873	B. F. Thomas
Geo. W. Maze	Aug. 22, 1870	B. F. Thomas
Josie Burgess	Dec. 23, 1874	B. F. Thomas
Alphonso Hickinson	Dec. 27, 1874	B. F. Thomas
Frank S. Sharp	Sep. --, 1874	B. F. Thomas
Thomas P. Clagett	Sep. --, 1874	B. F. Thomas
Mrs. Jennie Semson	Sep. --, 1874	B. F. Thomas
Mrs. Emma Wolf	Sep. --, 1874	B. F. Thomas
Sarah R. R. Frelden	Dec. 20, 1875	B. F. Thomas
Noah Hickerson	Aug. 8, 1877	S. H. McKlane
Robert C. Frelden	Aug. 8, 1877	S. H. McKlane
A. F. McCall	Aug. 8, 1877	S. H. McKlane
J. C. Hubbard	Aug. 8, 1877	S. H. McKlane
Joseph Orkins	Aug. 12, 1877	G. L. Moad
Mrs. Fannie Orkins	Aug. 12, 1877	G. L. Moad
Master F. A. Whitenack	Aug. 12, 1877	G. L. Moad
Miss M. F. Moore	Jul. 29, 1877	S. H. McElvain
Mrs. Mary F. Maize	Nov. 17, 1878	Y. W. Whitsett
George W. Brown	Nov. 17, 1878	Y. W. Whitsett
Mr. C. R. Rice	Nov. 24, 1878	Y. W. Whitsett
Miss Virginia Winehope	Nov. 24, 1878	Y. W. Whitsett
William Hinton	Nov. 20, 1879	J. Cal. Littrell
Mr. M. R. Glasgow	Nov. 20, 1879	J. Cal. Littrell
Mrs. Sarah A. Hinkle	Nov. 20, 1879	J. Cal. Littrell

Name	Date	Reverend
Walter Nickelson	Nov. 20, 1879	J. Cal. Littrell
John R. Hinkle	Nov. 20, 1879	J. Cal. Littrell
James Hinkle	Nov. 20, 1879	J. Cal. Littrell
John L. Moore	Nov. 20, 1879	J. Cal. Littrell
Miss Sarah H. Jones	Nov. 20, 1879	J. Cal. Littrell
Miss Della Hickerson	Nov. 20, 1879	J. Cal. Littrell
Miss Belle Hickerson	Nov. 20, 1879	J. Cal. Littrell
Bettie Moore	Dec. 7, 1879	J. Cal. Littrell
Mary J. Boling	Dec. 7, 1879	J. Cal. Littrell
Katie Guion	Jan. 2, 1881	J. H. Houx
Ida V. Mills	Nov. 4, 1881	J. H. Houx
Luie Casey	Nov. 14, 1881	J. H. Houx
Sarah O. Elliott	Nov. 14, 1881	J. H. Houx
Minnie Lee Casey	Nov. 14, 1881	J. H. Houx
Minnie A. Eagleson	Nov. 14, 1881	J. H. Houx
Lottie M. Mills	Nov. 14, 1881	J. H. Houx
Mary E. Smith	Nov. 14, 1881	J. H. Houx
Mattie A. Eagleson	Nov. 14, 1881	J. H. Houx
Eugene Wolff	Nov. 14, 1881	J. H. Houx
Thomas W. Moore	Nov. 14, 1881	J. H. Houx
Llewellyn G. Wolff	Nov. 14, 1881	J. H. Houx
John S. Casey	Nov. 14, 1881	J. H. Houx
Sarah Holt	Dec. 4, 1881	J. H. Houx
John W. Bond	Nov. 5, 1882	J. H. Houx
Francis E. Comer	Sep. 11, 1885	J. B. Fly
H. J. Cook	Sep. 11, 1885	J. B. Fly
Elmo Maize	Sep. 11, 1885	J. B. Fly
Jasper N. Cale	Sep. 11, 1885	J. B. Fly
Anna Barragar	Sep. 11, 1885	J. B. Fly
Andrew M. Comer	Sep. 13, 1885	Z. T. Orr
Clarance McCann	Sep. 13, 1885	Z. T. Orr
Jennie Bemis	Sep. 13, 1885	Z. T. Orr
Robert Hawkins	Aug. 29, 1886	Z. T. Orr
Walter Runner	Aug. 29, 1886	Z. T. Orr
Moses E. Watkins	Aug. 29, 1886	Z. T. Orr
James M. Barrager	Aug. 29, 1886	Z. T. Orr
Daniel Barrager	Aug. 29, 1886	Z. T. Orr
Sarah E. Watkins	Aug. 29, 1886	Z. T. Orr
Carrie L. McCann	Aug. 29, 1886	Z. T. Orr
Zerelda Barrager	Sep. 1, 1886	Z. T. Orr
James H. Roser	Sep. 1, 1886	Z. T. Orr
Maggie S. Whittaker	Sep. 2, 1886	Z. T. Orr
Ida Whittaker	Sep. 2, 1886	Z. T. Orr
John W. Hood	Sep. 5, 1886	Z. T. Orr
Della Hood	Sep. 5, 1886	Z. T. Orr
Georgia E. Whitside	Sep. 12, 1886	Z. T. Orr
Cynthia N. Bailey	Sep. 12, 1886	Z. T. Orr
Della M. Bailey	Sep. 12, 1886	Z. T. Orr

Name	Date	Reverend
James Bailey	Sep. 12, 1886	Z. T. Orr
Allice (sic) Moore	Sep. 11, 1887	Z. T. Orr
Effa Casey	Sep. 11, 1887	Z. T. Orr
Clara A. Wade	Sep. 11, 1887	Z. T. Orr
Bertha Watkins	Sep. 11, 1887	Z. T. Orr
Lulia Watkins	Sep. 11, 1887	Z. T. Orr
Ella Wolff	Sep. 11, 1887	Z. T. Orr
Samuel T. Lycook	Sep. 11, 1887	Z. T. Orr
Thomas Hincher	Sep. 11, 1887	Z. T. Orr
George W. Elliott	Sep. 11, 1887	Z. T. Orr
Luella Murray	Sep. 7, 1888	Z. T. Orr
Ada G. Smith	Sep. 7, 1888	Z. T. Orr
Anna M. Tilman	Sep. 7, 1888	Z. T. Orr
Eli D. Bradshaw	Sep. 9, 1888	Z. T. Orr
Melissa C. Webb	Sep. 9, 1888	Z. T. Orr
Clara V. Hicks	Sep. 9, 1888	Z. T. Orr
M. C. Dunn	Sep. 10, 1888	Z. T. Orr
Wm. R. Hicks	Sep. 11, 1888	Z. T. Orr
Lucy M. Casey	Nov. 24, 1890	Z. T. Orr
Lullie Moore	Nov. 24, 1890	Z. T. Orr
Annie Lee Casey	Nov. 24, 1890	Z. T. Orr
Cliff H. Kensinger	Nov. 24, 1890	Z. T. Orr
George Barker	Nov. 24, 1890	Z. T. Orr
Frank Trissemiter	Nov. 27, 1890	Z. T. Orr
Laura Trissemiter	Nov. 27, 1890	Z. T. Orr
Mattie E. Andrew	Nov. 27, 1890	Z. T. Orr
Clara E. Bradshaw	Nov. 27, 1890	Z. T. Orr
Etta M. Bradshaw	Nov. 27, 1890	Z. T. Orr
Minnie Wade	Nov. 27, 1890	Z. T. Orr
Merodith Wade	Nov. 27, 1890	Z. T. Orr
Lena Tilman	Nov. 30, 1890	Z. T. Orr
Warren Wickham	Nov. 30, 1890	Z. T. Orr
James Heckter	Dec. 20, 1891	Z. T. Orr
Allice (sic) Bailey	Nov. 20, 1892	Z. T. Orr
Dora Snodgrass	Nov. 20, 1892	Z. T. Orr
Della Wade	Nov. 20, 1892	Z. T. Orr
Miss Lise Gains	Aug. 8, 1894	Z. T. Orr
Etta M. Powers	Nov. 2, 1894	L. R. Nichols
George F. Crooks	Nov. 2, 1894	L. R. Nichols
James C. Commer	Nov. 2, 1894	L. R. Nichols
George W. Comer (sic)	Nov. 2, 1894	L. R. Nichols
John H. E. Elliott	Nov. 2, 1894	L. R. Nichols
Henry C. Descombs	Dec. 23, 1894	L. R. Nichols
John W. Woolf	Dec. 23, 1894	L. R. Nichols
Albert Scott	Sep. 20, 1894	B. Margeson
Lewis F. Waldridge	Sep. 20, 1894	B. Margeson
John C. Whiteman	Sep. 22, 1895	B. Margeson
Lela J. H. Elliott	Sep. 23, 1895	B. Margeson

Name	Date	Reverend
Mary Hathaway	Sep. 23, 1895	B. Margeson
Wm. W. Bailey	Sep. 23, 1895	B. Margeson
Roy Whitesides	Jul. --, 1895	L. R. Nichols
Edward Bailey	Jul. --, 1895	L. R. Nichols
J. G. Beaty	Sep. 30, 1895	L. R. Nichols
Miss Hattie Lewis	Sep. 30, 1895	L. R. Nichols
Lewis Bradley	Jun. 21, 1896	Y. W. Whitsett

Register of Deaths

Name (Deceased)	Death Date	Reverend/Service
James Kimsey	Jul. 9, 1870	---
Mrs. Martha J. Hays	Feb. 23, 1872	---
Mrs. Cary Baker	Aug. 17, 1876	B. F. Thomas
Mrs. Nancy Murray	Feb. 12, 1879	Y. W. Whitsett
Marietta Whitworth	Mar. 27, 1888	Z. T. Orr
Jane Morgart	Feb. 12, 1887	J. A. Murphey

Register of Marriages

Cary Allen Eager and Margaret Jane Wade, (MD) July 31, 1870, (JP) J. H. McCann.

Ferdinan Crooks and Mary DaComb, (MD) November 27, 1872, (MG) B. F. Thomas.

Frank S. Sharp and Nancy E. Evans, (MD) December 3, 1874, (MG) B. F. Thomas.

George W. Maize and Sallie W. Martin, (MD) December 17, 1874, (MG) B. F. Thomas.

W. L. Roy and Mary A. Davis, (MD) December 31, 1874, (MG) B. F. Thomas.

John B. Barker and Carrie L. Powers, (MD) May 6, 1875, (MG) B. F. Thomas.

Henry Hinton and Susan Kimsey, (MD) October 17, 1875, (MG) B. F. Thomas.

Wm. Tuttle and Mrs. Jemina Darling, (MD) July 20, 1875, (MG) B. F. Thomas.

Wm. Whitworth and Mrs. Marideth Crooks, (MD) Not given, (MG) J. H. Gillespie.

J. R. Maize and Mary Neal, (MD) Not Given, (MG) B. F. Thomas.

John R. Barker and Amanda E. Casey, (MD) November 27, 1879, (MG) B. F. Thomas.

Thomas Zarnes and Mattie A. Eagleson, (MD) Not given, (MG) S. Finis King.

David Williamson and Elizabeth Sharp, (MG) Z. T. Orr.

C. H. Kensinger and Minnie Eagleson, (MD) January 28, 1891, (MG) Z. T. Orr.

Johnson Kensinger and Clara A. Wade, (MD) Mar. --, 1892, (MG) Z. T. Orr.

Register of Elders

Name	Ceased to Act	Ordained
P. W. Moore	---	1850

Name	Ceased to Act	Ordained
Daniel Grey	Sep. --, 1876	Feb. 20, 1876
Mosses (sic) E. Watkins	---	---
--- Fitzwater	Mar. --, 1873	---
Saml. H. Elliott	---	Sep. 20, 1874
Geo. W. Maize	Mar. 9, 1878	Sep. 20, 1874
John W. Brouagh	---	Mar. 5, 1882
Robert Sharp	---	Mar. 5, 1882
G. W. Watkins	---	Feb. 22, 1894
Frank S. Sharp	May 18, 1878	Mar. 12, 1876
Llewellyn Woolff	---	Feb. 22, 1891
Dr. J. G. Beaty	---	Nov. 8, 1897
Wm. Hinton	---	Nov. 8, 1897
C. L. Crooks	---	Nov. 8, 1897

Register of Deacons

Name	Ceased to Act	Ordained
Geo. M. Casey	---	Sep. 20, 1874
Ferdinan Crooks	---	Sep. 20, 1874
Andrew Russell	Mar. 11, 1877 (died)	Sep. 20, 1874
Jacob Wolf	---	Mar. 12, 1876
James Eagleson	Mar. 1, 1895	Mar. 5, 1882
Wm. Hinton	Nov. 8, 1897	Mar. 5, 1882
Mrs. Wm. Hinton	---	Nov. 8, 1897
Alice Powers	---	Nov. 8, 1897

Register of Infant Baptisms

Sallie A. Whitsett, (PRTS) Mr. and Mrs. Y. W. Whitsett, (BD) November 19, 1878, (MG) W. W. Brannum.

Olive B. Maize, (PRTS) Mr. and Mrs. J. R. Maize, (BD) November 19, 1878, (MG) W. W. Brannum.

Charles L. Crooks, (PRTS) Mr. and Mrs. F. M. Crooks, (BD) November 19, 1878, (MG) W. W. Brannum.

George F. Crooks, (PRTS) Mr. and Mrs. F. M. Crooks, (BD) November 19, 1878, (MG) W. W. Brannum.

Delia A. Crooks, (PRTS) Mr. and Mrs. F. M. Crooks, (BD) November 19, 1878, (MG) W. W. Brannum.

William Sharp, (PRTS) Robert and Alice Sharp, (BD) February 28, 1888, (MG) Z. T. Orr.

Joseph Sharp, (PRTS) Robert and Alice Sharp, (BD) February 28, 1888, (MG) Z. T. Orr.

Ava Lee Hinton, (PRTS) Wm. and Lizzie L. Hinton, (BD) November 24, 1890, (MG) Z. T. Orr.

Emeline Hinton, (PRTS) Wm. and Lizzie L. Hinton, (BD) November 24, 1890, (MG) Z. T. Orr.

Fannie S. Nichols, (PRTS) Rev. L. R. and Hattie M. Nichols, (BD) August 8, 1894, (MG) Z. T. Orr,

Edna Isabella Kensinger, (PRTS) Mr. and Mrs. Johnson Kensinger, (BD) September 7, 1897, (MG) J. A. Murphy

Building Fund Pledges, March 23, 1871

G. M. Casey, Philip W. Moore, Wm. Adair, John R. Powers, F. W. Crooks, Joseph Sharp, J. H. McCann, Wm. Tuttle, Danl. Grey, George W. Murray, F. W. Bleil, W. T. Wilson, D. B. Whidbee, C. E. Powers, Geo. Arnold, William Paul, William Hinton, John Woolfolk, William P. Moore, Bedford Tuttle, Frank Crooks, Frank Kemp, Charles DesCombs, Joseph Williams, Jane Stone, William J. Ferel, William Freeland, D. B. Lambert, Isaac Adair, N. B. Moore, Robert Harwood, David Snodgrass, Rebecca Neil, V. J. Moore, Jacob Thrasher, Jacob Fingle, Sarah Kimsay, Robert Sharp, Senr., P. DesCombs, Max McCann, Mary F. Moore, H. Caldwell, Frank Caldwell, D. P. Kimsey, M. E. Watkins, Joseph Cole, Jas. H. Carter, John Coppage, Willis Helm, Joseph Berger, W. D. Wash, Elias Tuttle, W. J. Butler, G. Townsler, R. C. Ceicil, Emma Wolff, A. Judge, W. A. Bryson, E. C. Gillam, N. H. Fitzwater, B. F. Thomas, W. E. Foster, P. R. Webster, J. D. Wiseman, Alexr. Miller, John J. Mason, A. J. Bailey, J. W. Harriger, G. Y. Salmon, Philip Land, D. C. Stone, F. H. Land, Jacob Wolff, John Curtis, A. C. Comer, Robt. Allen, Herkett & Brother, John Ragland, Ed Curtis, H. Riehl, N. D. Land, Haysler & Brother, B. L. Quarrels, E. A. Covington, Geo. Barker, Salmon & Stone, S. D. Garth, F. W. McFarland, W. G. Rogers, --- McCollins, R. W. Cressy, Wm. S. Stone, B. G. Boone, Roberts & Bro., Jas. Webb, Robert Lewis, Jacob Goldsmith, Andrew Russell, R. B. Smith, R. T. Lindsey, Robt. Gilbert, Miles Weeks, R. B. Casey, John A. Townsend, Sarah Jane Holt, Y. G. Culley, Jack Johnson, John C. Culley, G. D. Wright, T. J. Wright, J. D. Farr, E. H. Askew, W. R. Culley, P. P. Embrey, Saml. R. Brown, John R. Johnson, W. P. Huff, Arthur Hand, W. J. McFarland, J. D. Willaimson, N. W. Norris, J. F. Loyd, S. V. Turner, D. W. Bennzette, Myron Wallace, T. N. Carpenter, R. R. Walls, Jas. G. Turk, W. S. Wantland.

Register of Communicants

Name	Admission Date	Dismissed Date
Mary Moore	Sep. 1869	---
Jane Kimsey	Sep. 1869	Jul. 7, 1870 died
Mary Jane Guion (Lamar)	Sep. 1869	Sep. 2, 1886
Elizabeth Sharp (Williamson)	Sep. 1869	---
Jane Ann Sharp	Sep. 1869	Dec. 12, 1890
Maryette Jane Wade	Sep. 1869	Mar. 1872
Ferdinan W. Crooks	Sep. 1869	---
Jesse Sharp	Sep. 1869	Dec. 12, 1890
George M. Casey	Sep. 1869	---
Philip W. Moore	Sep. 1869	---
Arminta Moore	Sep. 1869	1881 - died 1884
Laneclin Fieland	Sep. 1869	---

Name	Admission Date	Dismissed Date
Nancy Murray	Nov. 1869	Feb. 12, 1879 died
Wm. Pleasant Moore	Nov. 1869	Sep. 1870 moved
Daniel Grey	Nov. 1869	Oct. 7, 1876 moved
Margrett Goings	Aug. 1870	Dec. 1873 moved in Aug. 1873
Martha J. Hays	Aug. 1870	Feb. 27, 1872 died
Julia T. Glasgow	Aug. 1870	Jan. 26, 1870
Jacop (sic) Goings	Aug. 1870	Dec. 1877 moved in Aug. 1877
Joseph Maize	Aug. 1870	May 9, 1885
Martha Grey	Aug. 1870	Dec. 5, 1884
Barlow Eskern	Aug. 1870	Oct. 31, 1870
*D. H. Fitzwater *(Moved March 1873)	Aug. 2872	Jan. 8, 1876
*E. H. Fitzwater *(Moved March 1873)	Aug. 1872	Jan. 8, 1876
Susan Kimsey (Hinton)	Aug. 1872	Oct. 7, 1875
Elizabeth C. Gillam	Aug. 1872	---
Cara Powers (Barker)	Aug. 1872	---
Joseph D. Wiseman	Aug. 1872	Aug. 1873 moved
Ann Wiseman	Aug. 1872	Aug. 1873 moved
*Andrew Russell *(Died, Age: 72 y, 7 m, 11 d)	Aug. 1872	*Mar. 11, 1877
Amanda Casey (Barker)	Aug. 1872	---
*Robert B. Smith *(Repeated immoral conduct)	Aug. 1872	Nov. 23, 1872
Margrett E. Smith	Aug. 1872	Nov. 23, 1872
Susan Crabtree	Aug. 1872	1875
Martha J. Ely	Aug. 1872	Mar. 1876
Moses E. Watkins	Aug. 1872	---
Nancy Jane Watkins	Aug. 1872	---
Mrs. David Prosser	---	---
Mary Caldwell (Stone)	---	Non-resident
Mary J. Crooks	Mar. 1873	---
Willis Helm	Jul. 1873	1873
Martha Helm	Jul. 1873	---
Francis M. Kimsey	Jul. 1873	1879
Susan Kimsey	Jul. 1873	1879
Mary P. McMahan	Aug. 1873	---
Lucy H. Casey	Aug. 1873	---
George Maize	Aug. 1873	1878
*William M. Whitworth *(Expelled)	Aug. 1873	Jun. 7, 1890
Anson A. Whitaker	Aug. 1873	Mar. 29, 1877
Mary C. Whitaker	Aug. 1873	Mar. 29, 1877

Name	Admission Date	Dismissed Date
Cary E. Davis	Aug. 1873	Mar. 1875
Mary A. Davis	Aug. 1873	1874
Cary Watkins (Brooks)	Aug. 1873	May 1886
Niel Tuttle	Sep. 11, 1874	Mar. 1876
Samuel H. Elliott	Sep. 11, 1874	---
Jacob Wolff	Sep. 11, 1874	---
Addiline Eagleson	Sep. 11, 1874	---
Elias Wolf	Sep. 11, 1874	---
Jeannie Simpson	Sep. 11, 1874	1879 moved in Mar. 1875
Elias Tuttle	Sep. 11, 1874	---
Francis Sharp	Sep. 11, 1874	1878
Thomas J. Clagett	Sep. 11, 1874	May 15, 1891
Mrs. Eliza Jane Johnson	Dec. 22, 1874	Oct. 28, 1881
George W. Glasgow	Dec. 23, 1874	Jan. 25, 1876
*Josie Burges	Dec. 23, 1874	Jun. 16, 1877
*(Found guilty of violation)		
Alphonso Hickerson	Dec. 27, 1874	1881
Sarah R. Fielden	Dec. 30, 1874	Aug. 1876 moved in Feb. 1876
Robert C. Fielden	Dec. 30, 1874	Aug. 1876 moved in Feb. 1876
Nancy E. Sharp	Dec. 16, 1875	---
Elizabeth Elder	Dec. 16, 1875	---
Syntha Kate Smith	Dec. 14, 1876	1877 moved in Sep. 1876
Mrs. Marcella Tingle	Aug. 18, 1876	Jun. 2, 1883
Mrs. Carrie Y. Elliott	Aug. 18, 1876	---
Rev. Y. W. Whitsett	Jul. 29, 1877	Jun. 30, 1883
Mattie Moore (Robins)	Jul. 29, 1877	Feb. 24, 1895
*Mrs. Mary Smith	Jul. 30, 1877	Jul. 9, 1880
*(Died, Age: 75y)		
Mr. J. C. Hubbard	Aug. 8, 1877	1878
F. McCall	Aug. 8, 1877	Nov. 28, 1875
Noah Hickerson	Aug. 1877	1879
Mrs. Jennie Whitsett	Aug. 1877	Jun. 30, 1883
*Joseph Oskins	Aug. 13, 1877	Dec. 19, 1898
*(Died, Transferred to Tebo Congregation)		
Mrs. Fannie Oskins	Aug. 13, 1877	Transferred to Tebo Congre.
Mrs. Whitmack	Aug. 13, 1877	Oct. 1, 1881
Mrs. Lydia Tingler	Aug. 13, 1877	1880
Mr. L. B. Lambert	Aug. 20, 1877	Nov. 23, 1878
Mrs. Mary F. Maize	Nov. 17, 1878	May 1885
Robert Sharp	Nov. 17, 1878	Feb. 27, 1888
George W. Brown	Nov. 17, 1878	1880
Mrs. C. R. Rice	Nov. 23, 1878	1879
Mr. J. M. Thompson	Nov. 23, 1877	---

Name	Admission Date	Dismissed Date
Mrs. P. Y. Rice	Nov. 23, 1878	---
Miss Virginia Wineholfe	Nov. 24, 1878	1881
James Eagleson	Nov. 20, 1879	---
Major Brown	Nov. 20, 1878	1885
Francis M. Land	Nov. 20, 1878	Dec. 15, 1893
Mrs. M. R. Glasgow	Nov. 20, 1879	1888 left the county
Mrs. S. F. Glasgow	Nov. 20, 1879	1893 moved
Mrs. Sarah A. Hinkle	Nov. 20, 1879	1894 moved
John R. Hinkle	Nov. 20, 1879	1894 moved
*Frank Crooks *(Suspended for unchristian conduct)	Nov. 20, 1879	Nov. 6, 1880
*Walter Nickelson *(Moved on Oct. 20, 1880, died 1881)	Nov. 20, 1879	Nov. 19, 1880
James Hinkle	Nov. 20, 1879	---
John L. Linstone	Nov. 20, 1879	Feb. 8, 1889 moved 1885
J. T. Jones	Nov. 20, 1879	1882 moved
Miss Sarah A. Jones	Nov. 20, 1879	moved
Amanda Hickerson	Nov. 20, 1879	moved
Della Hickerson	Nov. 20, 1879	moved
Bella Hickerson	Nov. 20, 1879	moved
Amanda E. Moore (Wolff)	Dec. 7, 1879	---
Mary J. Boling	Dec. 7, 1879	*Feb. 1, 1888 *(died)
Margaret E. Smith	May 1, 1880	Mar. 8, 1889
*Robert B. Smith *(Suspended)	May 1, 1880	Mar. 12, 1887
*Sarah D. Elliott *(Died Jul. 14, 1886)	Nov. 7, 1880	Jun. 8, 1883
Leonia Eager	Jan. 1, 1881	Jun. 30, 1883
Dr. J. W. Bronaugh	Jun. 25, 1881	Feb. 19, 1884
Katie Guion	Jun. 2, 1881	Joined Baptists
Miss Ida V. Miller	Nov. 4, 1881	Feb. 19, 1894
Sallie McCann	Nov. 6, 1881	---
Julia Casey (Kingsberry)	Nov. 14, 1881	---
Minnie Lee Casey (Hughes)	Aug. 14, 1881	Jun. 21, 1877
*John C. Casey *(Expelled)	Aug. 14, 1881	Sep. 1886
*Sarah O. Elthel *(Descombs)	Aug. 14, 1881	Apr. 1893
Minnie H. Eagleson *(Kensinger)	Aug. 14, 1881	---
*Mollie A. Eagleson *(Zarnes)	Aug. 14, 1881	---
Lottie M. Mills	Aug. 14, 1881	Jun. 2, 1883
Millie A. Mills	Nov. 15, 1881	---
*Mary E. Smith (Atchison)	Nov. 15, 1881	---

Name	Admission Date	Dismissed Date
Eugene Wolf	Nov. 15, 1881	Aug. 12, 1887
Llwellyn G. Wolf	Nov. 15, 1881	---
Thomas W. Moore	Nov. 15, 1881	Aug. 12, 1887
Abner E. Adair	Nov. 15, 1881	Dec. 22, 1888
*Sarah Holt	Dec, 4, 1881	Aug. 4, 1883
*(Suspended for immoral conduct)		
Mary Allice (sic) Eagleson (Powers)	Dec. 4, 1881	---
John W. Bond	Nov. 5, 1882	Aug. 8, 1885
Joseph Nash	Dec. 9, 1883	1885
Mary E. Nash	Dec. 9, 1883	1885
Francis E. Comer	Sep. 11, 1885	Aug. 8, 1890
H. J. Cook	Sep. 11, 1885	Oct. 1886
Jasper N. Cale	Sep. 11, 1885	May 8, 1886
Elmo Maizo	Sep. 11, 1885	1894
Anna Barrager (Reid)	Sep. 11, 1885	1894
Andrew M. Commer	Sep. 13, 1885	Aug. 8, 1890
Clarance McCann	Sep. 13, 1885	Jan. 15, 1892
Jennie Bemis	Sep. 13, 1885	1885
Mrs. Allice Kinsinger	Mar. 14, 1886	---
W. F. Guion	May 9, 1886	1887
*Nellie U. Clark	May 9, 1886	May 12, 1894
*(Moved in 1889)		
Jane Morgart	May 9, 1886	*Feb. 12, 1897
*(Died)		
A. Morris	Aug. 29, 1886	1889
Walter Runner	Aug. 29, 1886	Feb. 1887
Robert Hankins	Aug. 29, 1886	Joined the Methodists
*Moses E. Watkins, Jr.	Aug. 29, 1886	Sep. 9, 1887
*(Suspended for immoral conduct)		
James M. Barragar	Aug. 29, 1886	1894
Daniel Barragar	Aug. 29, 1886	Dec. 12, 1890
Sarah E. Watkins	Aug. 29, 1886	Oct. 4, 1894
Carrie L. McCann	Aug. 29, 1886	---
Zerelda Barrager	Sep. 1, 1886	---
James H. Roser	Sep. 1, 1886	Aug. 12, 1887
*Miss B. A. Orr	Sep. 1, 1886	*Dec. 29, 1890
*(Died, wife of Rev. Z. T. Orr)		
Maggie S. Whittaker	Sep. 2, 1886	Aug. 1883
*Ida Whittaker	Sep. 2, 1886	Dec. 6, 1896
*(Joined the Methodists)		
Cyntha N. Bailey	Sep. 5, 1886	---
Ellia S. Hammons	Sep. 5, 1886	---
John W. Hood	Sep. 5, 1886	---
Della Hood	Sep. 5, 1886	Oct. 12, 1896
Anna H. Tilman	Sep. 8, 1886	Feb. 3, 1888 died

Name	Admission Date	Dismissed Date
George W. Whitsides	Sep. 8, 1886	---
Della M. Bailey	Sep. 8, 1886	---
James Bailey	Sep. 8, 1886	---
Elizabeth A. Watkins	Sep. 8, 1886	---
Marietta Whitworth	Sep. 8, 1886	Mar. 26, 1888 died
William H. Hammons	Oct. 9, 1886	---
Lottie Main	Nov. 14, 1886	1888
George W. Rondel	Nov. 28, 1886	---
Harriett Rondel	Nov. 28, 1886	Apr. 1898
John L. Descombs	Dec. 12, 1896	Jan. 6, 1893 died
James Webb	Jun. 26, 1887	---
Elizabeth Webb	Jul. 24, 1887	---
Allice (sic) Moore	Sep. 8, 1887	---
Effa Casey	Sep. 8, 1887	---
Clara A. Wade *	Sep. 8, 1887	*(Kensinger)
Bertha Whitsides	Sep. 8, 1887	---
Lula Watkins	Sep. 8, 1887	Oct. 4, 1894
Effa Wolff	Sep. 8, 1887	---
Samuel T. Laycock	Sep. 8, 1887	Mar. 6, 1894
Charles Crooks	Sep. 8, 1887	---
Thomas Hincher	Sep. 8, 1887	Jan. 10, 1890
George W. Elliott	Sep. 8, 1887	Mar. 2, 1894
Martha A. Wade	Sep. 8, 1887	---
L. D. Wade	Sep. 8, 1887	---
Mary L. Orr	Sep. 8, 1887	May 12, 1894
Ella Whitsides (Crow)	Sep. 8, 1887	Aug. 8, 1888
Jones A. Orr	Sep. 8, 1887	May 12, 1894
Emily Whitsides	Sep. 8, 1887	Aug. 12, 1891 died
Rusinlee Dunaway	Sep. 25, 1887	1890
Mary E. Webb (Orr)	Nov. 13, 1887	May 12, 1894
Cora J. Webb (Ragland)	Nov. 13, 1887	Aug. 1893
Luella Murray (Baker)	Sep. 7, 1888	Aug. 1883
Ada F. Smith	Sep. 7, 1888	Sep. 11, 1901 moved in 1890
Anna M. Tilman	Sep. 7, 1888	---
Mrs. Bridget Powers	Sep. 8, 1888	---
Manerva E. Evans	Sep. 8, 1888	Dec. 22, 1888
Matilda E. Smith	Sep. 8, 1888	1890 moved to Warrensburg
Wm. H. Bradshaw	Sep. 9, 1888	1889 moved
Melissa C. Webb *	Sep. 9, 1888	*(McQuitten)
Clara V. Hicks	Sep. 9, 1888	---
M. C. Dunn	Sep. 10, 1888	Oct. 17, 1891
Sarah Ford	Sep. 11, 1888	1889
Lucy Bailey	Sep. 11, 1888	1890 moved

Name	Admission Date	Dismissed Date
Sarah E. Bailey	Sep. 11, 1888	Nov. 13, 1891 moved in 1890
Lucy Bailey	Sep. 11, 1888	1890 moved
Frank H. Ford	Sep. 11, 1888	1890 moved
Wm. R. Hicks	Sep. 11, 1888	Moved out of bounds
J. W. Wright	Mar. 23, 1889	---
Martha F. Wright	Mar. 23, 1889	---
Mrs. Wilhemia F. Redford	Mar. 23, 1889	---
Lizza L. Hinton	Apr. 28, 1889	---
Miss Emma McDorman	Dec. 22, 1889	Nov. 18, 1893
Eugene Wolff	Dec. 22, 1889	May 12, 1894
Lucy M. Casey	Nov. 24, 1890	May 12, 1894
Annie Lee Casey	Nov. 24, 1890	---
Lullie Moore	Nov. 24, 1890	---
Lizzie A. Hinton (Moore)	Nov. 24, 1890	---
Y. N. Watkins	Nov. 24, 1890	---
Cliff H. Kinsinger	Nov. 24, 1890	Dec. 15, 1893
George Barker	Nov. 24, 1890	1892
Charles H. Cameron	Nov. 27, 1890	Nov. 16, 1894
Lewis H. Kinsinger	Nov. 27, 1890	Jul. 7, 1893 died
Frank Tressinriter	Nov. 27, 1890	---
Laura Tressinriter	Nov. 27, 1890	---
Mattie E. Andrew	Nov. 27, 1890	---
Clara E. Bradshaw	Nov. 27, 1890	---
Etta M. Bradshaw	Nov. 27, 1890	---
Minnie Wade	Nov. 27, 1890	---
Merredith Wade	Nov. 27, 1890	---
Lena E. Orr	Nov. 27, 1890	May 12, 1894
James Tilman	Nov. 30, 1890	1892 moved
Warren Wickham	Nov. 30, 1890	1891
A. M. Tilman	Dec. 14, 1890	1893
G. L. Ball	Sep. 26, 1891	Oct. 17, 1891
Ann E. Ball	Sep. 26, 1891	Oct. 17, 1891
Lizzie M. Ball	Sep. 26, 1891	Oct. 17, 1891
Jennie Holton	Sep. 26, 1891	1892
Thomas B. Holton	Sep. 26, 1891	Oct. 1894 joined Methodists
Dora A. Hammar	Dec. 11, 1891	---
James Heckter	Dec. 11, 1891	1892
Mary Hecktor	Dec. 11, 1891	1892
Annie Fenley	Dec. 20, 1891	1892
Una B. Watkins	Sep. 26, 1892	---
Cora E. Comer	Sep. 26, 1892	Dec. 15, 1893
Nora Wade	Sep. 26, 1892	1892 moved
Ola Smith	Sep. 26, 1892	---
Allice (Sic) Bailey	Sep. 30, 1892	---

Name	Admission Date	Dismissed Date
Della Crooks	Sep. 30, 1892	---
Della Wade	Oct. 4, 1892	Dec. 15, 1893
Dora Snodgrass (Bailey)	Oct. 16, 1892	---
Mrs. Georgie Bronaugh	Sep. 2, 1893	Feb. 18, 1894
Miss Lue Gains	Nov. 13, 1893	Oct. 4, 1894
Mrs. Hattie M. Nichols	Aug. 8, 1894	Jul. 5, 1896
F. E. Comer	Nov. 1, 1894	---
Etta M. Wolff (Powers)	Nov. 2, 1894	Nov. 1876
Lula Wade	Nov. 2, 1894	---
George F. Crooks	Nov. 2, 1894	---
John H. C. Elliott	Nov. 2, 1894	---
James C. Comer	Nov. 2, 1894	Feb. 24, 1895
George W. Comer	Nov. 2, 1894	Feb. 24, 1895
Johnathan Morgart	Dec. 23, 1894	---
Henry C. Descombs	Dec. 23, 1894	---
Roy Whitsides	Dec. 23, 1894	---
George W. Elliott	Dec. 23, 1894	---
John W. Woolf	Dec. 23, 1894	---
George Hathaway	Mar. 3, 1895	---
Huffman Landon	Sep. 20, 1895	---
Amanda Landon	Sep. 20, 1895	---
Olive Effie Landon	Sep. 20, 1895	---
Lewis G. Waldridge	Sep. 20, 1895	---
Albert Scott	Sep. 20, 1895	---
John C. Whiteman	Sep. 22, 1895	---
Miss Hattie Lewis	Sep. 23, 1895	---
Miss Mary Hattaway	Sep. 23, 1895	---
William W. Bailey	Sep. 23, 1895	---
Samuel T. Laycock	Sep. 23, 1895	---
Lela J. H. Elliott	Sep. 23, 1895	---
Mrs. Allice H. Morgart	Sep. 23, 1895	---
J. G. Beaty	Sep. 23, 1895	---
C. C. Bradley	Oct. 13, 1895	---
John W. Clark	Aug. 16, 1896	---
Ida M. Clark	Aug. 16, 1896	---
Mrs. John Dunaway	Unknown	

Cave Spring Cumberland Presbyterian Church, Cave Spring, Overton County, Tennessee
October 22, 1836, p. 2

Jobe Carlock, Abraham Hayter, John M'Donnald, Susannah L. M. Lansdon (d. Feb. 4, 1841), Judeth Lansden, Elizabeth Carlock, B. L. Carlock, Polly Hayter, Sarah Copeland, Andrew T. Hayter, Eliza Hayter (Carlock), Wm. T. Hayter, Robt. L. Ferril, Polly McDonnold, Thomas C. McDonnold, John J. Hayter, Thomas Hayter, Eleanor Ferril, Charlotte Ferril, Sally Hunt, Nelson F. Harward, Eliza Ann Harward, Alfred Tate, Margaret Hunt, Wm. McDonnold, Susannah McDonnold, Mary Ann Harward,

Anna Hites, Alsey Jackson, Lucinda Elder, John Smith, Thos. K. McDonnold, Catharine Hayter, Catharine Smith, Tabitha Lee, Merril Ledbetter, Sarah McDonnold (Hayter), Polley Ledbetter (Quales), Lucinda M'Ky (sic)(Lemmins), Wm. M. Martin, Campbell Hayter, Nancy Martin, Robert Coleman, Donna Taylor, Mgaries (?) Johnston, Polly Stewart, Job Carlock, Jr., Evan Campbell, Quintin Elder, Samuel Tate, Dawson Jackson, Silas Lemans, Benjamin McDonnold, Sussannah Smith, Catherine Worley, Saomi Worley, Rebeckah Worley, Elizabeth J. Carlock, Florah M'Millan, Mary Martin, Margaret McMillon, Nancy C. Bates, Jane McMillon, James S. Lansdon, Fanney Ledbetter, Libuton D. Hayter, Harriet J. McDonnold, Carline Means, F. J. Robbins, Sarah McDonnold (woman of colour), James Johnson, Carline Martin (woman of colour), Margaret Ledbetter, B. H. Ledbetter, Nancy Ledbetter (Jones), Rollings H. Johnson.

July, 1840, p. 46

Robert Coleman was charged with immoral conduct and suspended. N. F. Howard, clerk.

September 25, 1840, p. 47

The following persons were baptized: Dawson Jackson, B. L. Carlock, Jacob Lemmons, Quinton Elder, Babary Lace, Jobe Carlock, Polly Jackson, Elizabeth Ledbetter, Louisa Hayter, A. Hayter, J. McDonnold, J. K. Lansden, Milton (a black boy). N. F. Howard, clerk.

March 7, 1841, p. 48

Mary Jane, infant of Wm. and Susan McDonnold was baptized by J. K. Lansden.

September 26, (?), p. 56

Infants Baptisted: William H. C. Baits, Wm. S. Carlock, Matilda Ann and Sarah Carlock, James McDonnold, Ebion E. Hayter, Nancy E. Cambell (sic), Mary J. McDonnol (sic).

Deaths, No Date, p. 57

Name	Date
William S. Hayter	September 31, 1836
Elizabeth Tate	June 29, 1833
Eleanor McDonnold	March 29, 1842
Rachel Wright	February 11, 1844
Judith Landen, consort of James K. Landen	April 17, 1844
Ann Hayter	September 6, 1844
Susannah E. L. Martin	February 6, 1849
Fanny Ledbetter, consort of Wm. Ledbetter	May 8, 1849
James Johnson	1851, in Missouri
Mary Worley	1851
Polly Hayter	December 5, 1866
Abraham Hayter	August 31, 1873

May 26, 1849, Membership List, p. 62

Thomas C. McDonnold, J. L. Dillard, Abram Hayter, John McDonnold, Ida Carlock (d. February 4, 1855), B. L. Carlock, R. & H. Johnston, John J. Hayter, Wm. Ledbetter, Elizabeth Carlock, Polly Hayter, Sarah Copeland, Elisa Carlock, Thomas M. Hayter, Wm. Hayter, Elizabeth Hayter, Robert L. Ferrill, Elenor Ferril, Charlotte Ferrill, Margaret Hunt, Robert Merdock, Keziah Hunt, Ailcey Jackson, Wm. Hayter, Jr., George Hayter, Arminty Hayter, Anna Ferrill, Lavina McDonnold, John Smith, Elizabeth McDonnold, Sally Hayter, Ingaver Johnson, Jonathan Hull, Nancy Hull, Polly Worley, Rebecca Worley, Wm. M. Martin, Laomi Worley, Permenis Coleman, Catharine Smith, Merril Ledbetter. Libern D. Hayter, Sarah D. Hayter, Nancy Martin, Lucinda Martin, Elizabeth Martin, Mary Anne Martin, Wm. Martin, Polly Stewart, Quinton Elder, Dawson Jackson, Charity C. Jackson, Silas Leman, Benjamin Leman, Susannah Hill, Catharine Howard, Margaret Cox, Harriet McDonnold, Elizabeth Carlock, Winfred V. Ledbetter, Carline C. Dillard, James C. Johnson (d. 1857), Sally Potete (Garret), Elizabeth J. Robbins, B. H. T. Ledbetter, Nancy Jones, Pheba L. Crawford (Good Hope Church, October 22, 1849), Elisa Robins, Wm. Couper, Susannah Cowper, Nancy Cowper, Richard Wallis, Menan Martin, John M. Carlock, Lemuel D. Carlock, Robert M. Hayter, Sarah Patric, Elizabeth Johnson, Simeon M. Crawford, Winfred Ledbetter, Newton D. Crawford, Abagail T. S. Crawford, Rebecca C. Paren, Mary J. Ledford, Martin E. Ledford, Elizabeth Alfred, Jones Ledbetter, Ivin Ledbetter, Elizabeth Ledbetter, John Robbins, Martin Robbins, James Robbins, Milly Ragan, Isaac B. Worley, R. K. Johnson, Jr., Franklin Elder, William Jones, Elcany (sic) Cooper, Elizabeth Craig, James Homes, Hiram G. Worley, Isaac Crawford.

1867, Membership List, p. 2

(Note: Pages were renumbered in the middle of the volume.)

A. Hayter, B. L. Carlock, David Crofford, Wm. Ledbetter, Roling H. Johnson, Sarah Copeland, Eliza Carlock, Elizabeth L. Martin, Sally Hunt, Hezieh Hunt, Robert Moredock, Lavina McDonnold, Sarah D. Hayter, Ann Ferril, Lucinda Martin, Mary Smith, Catharine Howard, Nancy Jones, Nancy Martin, Menan M. Martin, Eliza McDonnold, Jane Ledbetter, Newton D. Crawford, Mary I. Ledbetter, John Robins, Martha Robins, Isaac B. Worley, William Jones, Hiram G. Worley, Hetty A. Neely, Marena Shelton, Eliza Shelton, Mary J. Organ, Elma Martin, Mary I. Carlock, Emma Roberts, Manerva Lea, Sarah Stephens, Mary I. Croford, Amy Luin, Andrew M. Carlock, Polly Croford, Polly Stewart, Emmeline Linder, Saml. A. J. White and wife, W. H. Dean Ledbetter, America Jones, Susan Livingston, Jane Owens, Patunce Bledsoe (Ferral), Joseph Copeland, Emmerson C. Reed, Peter J. Meyers, Catharine Johnson, Nelly Cravens, Hester Hager, Mary J. Hayter, Dealy Shepherd, Armilda Dial, Luelly

Cullam (consort of A. M. Carlock, Talitha Coleman, John Singleton, Sells McDonnold, Thomas Johnson, John Worley, Henry Hagar, Polk Ledbetter John Robbins, jr., James Worley, Jas. B. Cox, Logan Shepard, Mikel Linder, Mac Ledbetter, Lafayette Ferril, Jane Ledbetter, Lam Ledbetter, George Crawford, John Bledsoe, Mary Tate, James H. Ferrill, Eva Ferrill, H. Z. Ferril, Martha Jones, Matilda Robbins (Evans), Victoria Carlock, Malinda Nealy, Leann Shepherd, Jesse Rooker, John Ledbetter, Center Brown, John Carr, Thomas Lenaman, Rueben Lenaman, Malissa Singleton, Alfred Robbins, Ann Linder, Mary Anne Worley, Fanne (sic) Sells (Robins), Martha Robins, Mary E. Smith, Margaret Ledbetter, Charity Smith, Lavina Worley, Dicy Owens, Nancy Worley, Lewis Newberg, Mandy Tally, Samuel Kiesling, William H. McDonnold, Mary R. Boofer (Worley), Nancy J. Ferral, Sarah Carlock, Myrenz Pendergrass, James H. Ferril, sr., John Irvin, Phebe Carr, Cintha Jones, Margaret S. Richardson (consort of M. N. Richard, b. May 21, 1873), Charles Keisling, Sarah Keisling, Manvera Crawford, Martha A. Ferrill, Margaret Ledbetter, Amanda Ledbetter, Sarah Smith.

Persons of Colour: Rose McDonnold, Sarah McDonnold, Caroline Martin, Mariah McDonnold.

March 7, 1874, Membership List, p. 150

David Crawford (d. June 11, 1875), B. L. Carlock, James B. Cox, James H. Ferril, Jr., A. M. Carlock, Joseph M. Copeland, E. L. Ferril, William Ledbetter, R. H. Johnson, Sarah Copeland, Eliza Carlock, Sally Hunt, Keziah Hunt, Ann Ferril, Levina McDonald, Sarah D. Hayter, Lucinda Martin, Jane D. Ledbetter, Elizabeth Martin, Mary Smith, Nancy Jones, S. F. White, Eliza McDonnold, M. M. Martin, Mary J. Ledbetter, John Robins, Martha Robins, Isaac B. Worley, Mary J. Organ, Wm. Jones, Hiram G. Worley, Hetty Ann Neely, Elmira Martin (Gilentine), Emerine Roberts, Mary J. Crawford (Lynch), S. A. J. White, America Jones (Joined Methodists), Patrina Bledsoe (Ferrill), Catharine Johnson (Smith), Mary J. Ledbetter, Nelly C. Owens, Dealy Shepard, Luelly Cullom, Hester Koger, John Singleton, J. S. McDonnold, T. F. Johnson, John Worley, Logan Shepard (d. 1875), J. Ledbetter, Manerva J. Ledbetter (Ruthasson), Matilda Organ, George Crawford, Mary Tate (Singleton), Eva Ferril, Matilda Robins (Joined the Cambellites), Maranda Neely, Francis Nebly (Ledbetter), Malinda Nelby, Victory Carlock (Fersling)(d. September 15, 1878), H. Z. Ferril, Leann Shephard, Isaac Copeland, John Cara, Martin Crowford, Laura Johnson, Alfred Robins (Evans), Mary A. Worley, Lavina Worley, Charity Smith, Nancy Worley, Margaret Guilford, Samuel Keilsling, Mary R. Boofer, Sarah E. Boofer, Manerva Robbins (joined the Baptists), Nancy J. Ferril, Myra Y. Pendergrass, John Irvin, James H. Ferril, Margaret Ledbetter, Amanda Ledbetter (Eldridge), Richard Winningham, Sarah Smith, Marena Shelton (Cain), Tabitha

Coleman, Eliza Shelton (Law), Peggy Pitman (wife of William Pittman), Nancy Martin, Armilda Ledbetter, Nancy J. Newley, Tary Gillingham, Monroe Sparksman, Sally Gillintine, Sally Templeton, Manerva Sparksman, H. C. Koger, D. D. Ferrill, Matilda Ferrill, Francis Organ, John Keisling, Mattie Smith, Jane Ledford, Gass Keilsing, Mary Ann Brown, Amanda Vaughn (Robins), Tennessee Vaughn (Ferrill), Sarah Owens (Vaughn), Lizzie Robins, John Leslie Winton, Margaret F. Jones, Nancy Walker, Arabelle Crawford (joined the Campbellites), Martha Ledbetter (Shephard), James Copeland, Alice German, Ervin Hayter, Ann Richards (Nealy), J. B. Allison, M. C. Alison, T. H. Ledbetter, G. Y. Richards, A. C. Hayter, John Smith, Isam Richards, Sarah Smith, Jane Lea (Belk), Mitchell Winton, Margaret Winton, J. C. Jones, M. L. Jones, S. B. Harrison, C. Harrison (McDonald), A. A. Harrison, Sarah Ledford, George Jones, David Mullins, Sibba Robins, Sarah Crawford, Winnie Ledbetter, Matilda Ann Smith, Samuel W. Nealy, Sarah Koger, Serrvil Ledbetter, K. P. Stewart (Dismissed August 29, 1878), Priety Stewart (Dismissed August 29, 1878), Mary Ann Crawford, Nathan Worley, Molley Hayter (Smith), Harriet Hayter, Elizabeth Biby (Keilsing), Mary Crawford, Forester Winton, John Ledford, K. Carlock, Alexander Kielsing, J. C. Eldridge, Anna Nettie Eldridge, Demetrius Copeland, Sarah Keilsing, jr. (sic), George Belk, James Vaughn, Thomas Carlock, Armilda Ledford, Grandison Ledford, Sarah Vaughn, Liza Farley, Lora German, Ann Hayter, Martha Smith, Sublima Carlock.

Huntsville Cumberland Presbyterian Church, Huntsville, Randolph County, Missouri

Register of Deacons

Name	Date Ordained
J. W. Hammett	Jul. 27, 1890

Register of Elders

Name	Date Ordained	Ceased to Act
M. Hammett	Jul. 27, 1890	---
W. Malone	---	---
W. Craven	Jul. 27, 1890	Jan. 10, 1893
Owen Craven	Apr. 23, 1893	Jan. 10, 1893
W. Manning	Feb. 24, 1895	Aug. --, 1899
A. Wood	Feb. 24, 1895	---

Register of Adult Baptisms

Name	Date	Reverend
Mrs. Sarah A. McLaughlin	Oct. 5, 1890	J. S. Howard
Garvin Jack	Dec. 7, 1890	J. S. Howard
Mrs. Stonie Ferrell	Feb. 22, 1891	J. S. Howard
Joseph M. Prior	Dec. 24, 1893	S. A. McPherson
Alice F. Prior	Dec. 24, 1893	S. A. McPherson
Lizie Williams	Mar. 23, 1895	J. T. Bacon
Perry Hartman	Dec. 13, 1896	T. S. Love

Name	Date	Reverend
Miss Hattie Burgstresser	May 15, 1898	C. L. Hiskett

Register of Deaths

Name	Died	Reverend
Mrs. Susan F. Malone	Sep. 8, 1890	J. S. Howard
G. H. Lowry	Jan. 22, 1898	E. B. Surface

Register of Communicants

Name	Admission Date
Owen Craven	Jul. 27, 1890
Mrs. Owen Craven (d. Feb. 14, 1910)	Jul. 27, 1890
J. K. Craven (d. May 14, 1910)	Jul. 27, 1890
J. W. Craven	Jul. 27, 1890
Mrs. Ida A. Craven	Jul. 27, 1890
J. W. Hammett	Jul. 27, 1890
Mrs. J. W. Hammett	Jul. 27, 1890
F. M. Hammett	Jul. 27, 1890
Mrs. Susan Hammett	Jul. 27, 1890
Miss Rebecca Hammett	Jul. 27, 1890
Mrs. Kate Kirkpatrick	Jul. 27, 1890
B. W. Malone	Jul. 27, 1890
Mrs. Susan Malone (d. Sep. 8, 1890)	Jul. 27, 1890
Mrs. Smith	Jul. 27, 1890
Mrs. Thomas (Dismissed May, 1896)	Jul. 27, 1890
J. S. Howard (Dismissed Jul. 27, 1891)	Jul. 27, 1890
Mrs. L. A. Howard (Dismissed 27, 1891)	Jul. 27, 1890
John Jack	Sep. 28, 1890
Mrs. Mary Jack	Sep. 28, 1890
Mrs. Stonie Terrell	Sep. 28, 1890
James McLauhlin	Oct. 5, 1890
Sarah A. McLaughlin	Oct. 5, 1890
Mrs. Lucy E. Williams	Nov. 2, 1890
Gavin Jack (Suspended Aug. 8, 1896)	Dec. 7, 1890
J. B. Carney (Dismissed May 23, 1892)	Oct. 19, 1890
Mrs. Fannie Carney (Dis. May 23, 1892)	Oct. 19, 1890
Mrs. Lutie Malone	Apr. 25, 1892
*Miss Fannie Smith	Jun. 26, 1892

*(Pastor would not emerse so she joined the Baptists.)

Rev. S. A. McPherson (Dis. Apr., 1894)	Nov. 13, 1892
Sister Addie McPherson (Dis. Apr.,1894)	Nov. 13, 1892
Peter Walker	May 28, 1893
Mrs. Mary Walker	May 28, 1893
Mary A. McPherson (Dismissed Apr., 1894)	Aug. 13, 1893
*Maggie Walker (Dismissed Aug. 8, 1896)	Dec. 24, 1893

*(Joined the Christian Church)

Joseph M. Prior	Dec. 24, 1893
Alice F. Prior	Dec. 24, 1896
W. A. Wood	Nov., 1894
Mrs. Lillie H. Wood	Nov., 1894

Name	Admission Date
Miss Jennie Bradney	Dec., 1894
John W. Manning	Feb. 24, 1895
Mrs. John W. Manning	Feb. 24, 1895
*Miss Elizabeth William	Mar. 23, 1895
*(Joined the M. E. Church)	
*Mary Jane Walker (Dismissed Aug. 8, 1896)	Apr. 21, 1895
*(Joined the Christian Church)	
Miss Maggie Jack	Apr. 21, 1895
Mrs. Allie Lowry (Dis. Oct. 12, 1896)	Jun. 2, 1895
Charles M. Tradway (Dismissed Jun., 1896)	Jun. 16, 1895
Perry Hartman	Dec. 13, 1896
Mrs. Eva Hartman	Dec. 13, 1896
G. H. Lowry (d. January 11, 1898)	Jan. 10, 1897
Mrs. Alle H. Lowry	Jan. 10, 1897
Miss Hattie Burgstusser	May 15, 1898
B. W. Malone (d. 1906)	---
Mrs. Lutie Malone (d. June, 1903)	Apr. 25, 1892

Revised Register of Communicants, December 19, 1898

J. W. Hammett, Mrs. Mary A. Hammett, F. M. Hammett (Married & moved), Mrs. Susan Hammett, Mrs. Kate Kirkpatrick (Moved to Yaes), Mrs. Calvin Smith (Moved to LaPlata, Mo), John Jack (Moved to Columbia, Mo), Mrs. Mary Jack, Mrs. Lillie H. Wood, Mrs. Stonie Jack, Mrs. Lucis E. Williams, Peter Walker, W. A. Wood, Miss Jennie Bradney, J. W. Manning, Mrs. J. W. Manning, Miss Maggie Jack, Mrs. Allie Lowry, Miss Hattie Burgstressor, Miss B. Slankard, J. H. Slankard, J. K. Craven, Mrs. Owen Craven, Owen Craven.

Prairie Grove Cumberland Presbyterian Church, Prairie Grove, Washington County, Arkansas

Register of Marriages

John Henson and Margaret J. Crawford, (MD) January 9, 1868, (MG) Rev. Thos. J. Smith.

Polk Haney and Tennessee R. Rollans, (MD) August 30, 1868, (MG) Rev. Wm. Newland.

John Buchanan and Julia Rice, (MD) December 30, 1868, (MG) Thos. Buchanan.

I. C. Shoftner and Sarah Bell Hartley, (MD) February 7, 1869, (MG) Rev. Peter Carnahan.

Alfred Manns and Rebecca J. SImpson, (MD) February 20, 1869, (MG) Wm. Newland.

J. I. Crawford and Lucy S. Norwood, (MD) November 28, 1869, (MG) Rev. John Buchanan.

Joseph Bandenby and Vandelia Branson, (MD) November 10, 1879, (MG) John Buchanan.

W. G. D. Hunds and A. Dallas Pittman, (MD) March 30, 1872, (MG) Rev. Saml. Black.

Robert P. Reed and Eveline Shofer, (MD) ?, (MG) Samuel

Black.
    Jas. Wasburn and Mary L. Reed, (MD) ?, (MG) Saml. Black.
    Albert Pollett and R. M. Shofer, (MD) ?, (MG) Samuel Black.
    Frank Parker and Alice Crawford, (MD) January 25, 1880.
    Rufus Staples and Nancy Johnston, (MD) February 7, 1884, (MG) Rev. B. F. Totten.
    Frank Pzeatt and M. E. Edmiston, (MD) ?, (MG) ?.
    Andrew Wilson and N. N. Cunningham, (MD) Octover 7, 1889, (MG) G. A. Henderson.
    --- Fox and Mary Carnson, (MD) August 20, 1893, (MG) G. A. Henderson.
    Clint Carl and Lizzie Rollans, (MD) March 16, 1893, (MG) Wm. Iyre.
    Aron Breates and Susie Cunningham, (MD) November 24, 1891, (MG) Rev. Lonford.
    Ben Shelby and Ruth Edminston, (MD) December --, 1892, (MG) P. Crozier.
    Wm. Campbell and Lillie Harrison, (MD) January 4, 1893, (MG) W. H. Dyer.
    Newl Cunningham and Miss Cook, (MD) December 15, 1896, (MG) J. H. Kelly.
    John Campbell and Mollie Nail, (MD) Novemmber --, 1896, (MG) J. G. Kelly.
    Wm. Campbell and Cora Bain, (MD) December 15, 1896, (MG) I. N. Harris.
    Dr. Jas. Pittman and Jennie McCormick, (MD) January 18, 1899, (MG) D. J. Weems.

Register of Infant Baptisms

Mattie Adele Crawford, (PRTS) J. P. and Lucy Crawford, (BD) May 25, 1872, (MG) Jno. Buchanan.
    Minnie Alvertie Crawford, (PRTS) J. P. and Lucy Crawford, (BD) July 27, 1873, (MG) Jno. Buchanan.
    Mary Cener Pittman, (PRTS) S. P. and S. D. Pittman, (BD) July 27, 1873, (MG) Jno. Buchanan.
    John Herbert Hinds, (PRTS), W. Y. D. and M. D. Hinds, (BD) July 27, 1873, (MG) Jno. Buchanan.
    Ethel Dallas Hinds, (PRTS) ?, (BD) ?, (MG) ?.
    Jas. Pittman, (PRTS) W. E. and H. C. Pittman, (BD) October 11, 1874, (MG) Jno. Buchanan.
    Ellis Pittman, (PRTS) W. E. and H. C. Pittman, (BD) October 11, 1874, (MG) Jno. Buchanan.
    Luella Reed, (PRTS) R. P. and Eveline Reed, (BD) October 11, 1874, (MG) Jno. Buchanan.
    William E. Pittman, (PRTS) W. E. and W. C. Pittman, (BD) August 10, 1879, (MG) F. R. Earle.
    Chas. Phillips, (PRTS) C. C. and Mary Phillips, (BD) August 10, 1879, (MG) F. R. Earle.
    Paul Cann, (PRTS) D. W. and J. E. Cann, (BD) August 31, 1890, (MG) F. R. Earle.

Alla Genet Cann, (PRTS) D. W. and J. E. Cann, (BD) September 17, 1893, (MG) G. A. Henderson.
Little Cann, (PRTS) D. W. and J. E. Cann, (BD) August 16, 1896, (MG) J. K. P. Crosier.
Little Kelley, (PRTS) J. H. and Annie Kelley, (BD) August 16, 1896, (MG) J. K. Crosier.
Willie Cann, (PRTS) D. W. and J. E. Cann, (BD) May 15, 1898, (MG) F. R. Earle.

Register of Deacons

Name	Ordained	Ceased to Act
S. R. Crawford	Dec. 15, 1867	1880
William R. Morrison	Sep. 11, 1880	1884
Jas. H. Bunch	Sep. 11, 1880	1885
Jesse Goddard	Sep. 11, 1880	Feb. 28, 1897

Register of Elders

Name	Ordained	Ceased to Act
W. D. Crawford	---	---
A. C. Smith	---	---
James A. Morton	May 22, 1859	d.Nov. 30, 1885
J. P. Carnahan	Dec. 15, 1867	---
John M. Reed	Dec. 15, 1867	---
W. G. D. Hinds	Feb. 16, 1868	---
Moses Rollans	Feb. 11, 1872	d.Jan. 22, 1882
B. F. Patton	Feb. 11, 1872	---
C. C. Phillips	Sep. 11, 1880	1885
J. P. Crawford	Sep. 11, 1880	1887
Jno. Campbell	Aug. 5, 1883	---
A. A. Evans	Aug. 5, 1883	1887
--- Wallace	May 20, 1888	Feb. 20, 1899
H. W. Scott	Feb. 17, 1889	---
R. P. Harrison	Aug. --, 1891	---
B. H. Harrison	Aug. --, 1894	---
D. W. Cann	Aug. --, 1894	---
N. Mallicoat	Aug. --, 1891	---

Register of Adult Baptisms

Name	Date	Reverend
Vandelia Brandenburg	Jan. 29, 1871	Saml. Black
Mary P. Marrs	Jan. 29, 1871	Saml. Black
Mary Hardy	Jan. 29, 1871	Saml. Black
Elvira F. Bunch	Aug. 20, 1871	Saml. Black
N. Elizabeth Bunch	Aug. 20, 1871	---
Eveline Sheaffer	Aug. 24, 1871	--- Ezelle
Rebecca M. Sheaffer	Aug. 24, 1871	--- Ezelle
Martha E. Marrs	Aug. 24, 1871	--- Ezelle
Martha H. Crawford	Aug. 24, 1871	--- Ezelle
Lucy Crawford	Aug. 24, 1871	--- Ezelle
Margaret Shoftner	Aug. 28, 1871	--- Ezelle
C. Cornelia Rish	Aug. 28, 1871	--- Ezelle

Name	Date	Reverend
Eliza Literal	Aug. 28, 1871	--- Ezelle
Ellen Buchanan	Sep. 10, 1871	Saml. Black
Joseph Tilly	Sep. 10, 1871	Saml. Black
J. Irvin Crawford	Jul. 27, 1873	Jno. Buchanan
Jesse Godard	Nov. 16, 1874	Jno. Buchanan
M. J. Permenter	Aug. 10, 1879	F. R. Earle
W. J. Wade	Aug. 10, 1879	B. F. Totton
C. H. Ranch	Aug. 10, 1879	B. F. Totton
Mary L. Gifford	Jun. 4, 1882	B. F. Totton
Loretta Durvin	Feb. 12, 1882	B. F. Totton
Nannie Cunningham	Nov. 27, 1888	G.A. Henderson
Bell Rollans	Nov. 27, 1888	G.A. Henderson
Maybell James	Nov. 27, 1888	G.A. Henderson
C. C. James	Dec. 16, 1888	G.A. Henderson
J. F. Wallis	Dec. 16, 1888	G.A. Henderson
H. E. Edmiston	Dec. 16, 1888	G.A. Henderson
Lizzie Rollans	Dec. 16, 1888	G.A. Henderson
Susan Cunningham	Dec. 16, 1888	G.A. Henderson
Mary Floyd	Dec. 16, 1888	G.A. Henderson
Deen Wallis	Dec. 16, 1888	G.A. Henderson
Ida Wallis	Dec. 16, 1888	G.A. Henderson
F. L. Phillips (sister)	Dec. 16, 1888	G.A. Henderson
Mary Brunk	Aug. 19, 1894	John Kelly
C. E. Cole	Aug. 19, 1894	John Kelly
Ellis Pittman	Aug. 30, 1894	John Kelly
Mary Edwards	May 17, 1886	John Kelly
Ada Loflin	May 17, 1886	John Kelly
U. S. Cole	Sep. 20, 1896	John Kelly
Nora Cole	Sep. 20, 1896	John Kelly
Alma Cole	Sep. 20, 1896	John Kelly
Tennie Cunningham	Sep. 20, 1896	John Kelly
Earl Cunningham	Sep. 20, 1896	John Kelly
Lillie Marrs	Sep. 20, 1896	John Kelly
C. M. Blakely	Sep. 20, 1896	John Kelly
J. M. Mitchel	Sep. 20, 1896	John Kelly
J. E. Harrison	Sep. 20, 1896	John Kelly
Jas. Wallace	Sep. 20, 1896	John Kelly
John Cole	Oct. 15, 1898	N. D. Hanks
Miss Mary Cole	Oct. 15, 1898	N. D. Hanks
Miss Rena Cole	Oct. 15, 1898	N. D. Hanks
Mrs. Dona Rollans	Oct. 15, 1898	N. D. Hanks

<u>Register of Communicants</u>

John B. Hardy, Caroline Hardy, Elizabeth A. Stevenson, G. A. Crawford, John Crawford, Martha Jane Crawford, Elizabeth Crawford, Lucinda Brandenburg, Arey Marrs, William Crawford, Celia Amanda Pierce, Robt. D. Crawford, Hannah Diven, Jacob D. Mayberry, Rossanna L. West (McPherson), James Marrs, Anna Marrs, Viney Marrs, Moses Rollans, Sarah Rollans, Margaret C.

Norwood, Jane Parsely, Alex. Marrs, Joseph Brandenberg, J. I. D. Hinds (AD. August 5, 1866), Mary Smith, Tennessee R. Rollans (Haines), Sally Crum, Nancy Pettigrew, Temple Marrs, Rhoda Hinds, M. Julia A. Hinds, Elizabeth P. Marrs, Mary P. Shoftner, Mary J. Borden, A. B. Neal, Sarah Borden, Carson M. Crawford, W. B. Reed, liza Borden, Cintha C. Sawyers, Elizabeth Sower, W. C. Crawford, Larenia Crawford, A. J. Young, Lucy Norwood (Crawford), Nancy Williams, Leonida Crawford, Martha J. Polson, N. C. Shoftner (AD. October 5, 1868), Julia Rice, (AD. October 5, 1868), Gabriel Softner (AD. October 5, 1868), P. W. Shoftner (AD. October 5, 1868), Hays C. Rollans, Thos. H. Crawford, James Ewing Edmiston, J. W. Job, Dizanna Young, Nancy Stevenson, Sarah Pittman, Mary G. Reed, Martha B. Reed, M. Dallas Pittman (Hinds), --- Job (2x)(sic), Sinai Buchannan (sic), Martha Buchanan, Leander Buchanan. Margeny Buchanan, John Buchanan, Lucy J. Neals, Elizabeth C. Crawford, Henrietta Stevenson, Rebecca J. Simpson (Hinds), William D. Crawford, A. Calvin Smith, James A. Morton, J. Preston Carnahan, G. D. Hinds, Vandelia Brandenburg (AD. November 13, 1870), Mary Jane Marrs (Godard, AD. November 13, 1870), Martha H. Crawford (Smith, AD. August 24, 1871), Mary Hardy (AD. November 13, 1870), B. F. Totton (AD. August, 1870), Eveline Sheaffer (Reed, AD. August 24, 1871), Rebecca M. Sheaffer (Tollett, AD. August 24, 1871), Mary E. Marrs (Mosby, AD. August 24, 1871), Lucy Crawford (Cruz, AD. August 24, 1871), John Steward (AD. August 20, 1871), Ellen Buchanan (AD. September 10, 1871), Joseph Tilly (AD. September 10, 1871), Ellen Buchanan (AD. November 10, 1871), Eliza Literal (AD. August 28, 1871), Martha Rogers, Margaret C. Pittman (AD. July 26, 1873), P. I. Crawford, William Thompson (AD. May 30, 1873), Charity Thompson (AD, May 30, 1873), Sarah Thompson (AD. May 30, 1873), Jesse Godard (Ad. August 16, 1873, G. W. Collins (Ad. August 16, 1873), Jane Collins (AD. August 16, 1873), Emma Crawford (AD. August 16, 1873), Mary Luck (AD. August 16, 1873), Mary V. Phillips (AD. August 10, 1879), W. J. Wade (AD. August 6, 1879), Mary Phillips (AD. August 10, 1873), Martha E. Wade (AD. August 6, 1879), Chas. P. Reed (AD. August 10, 1879), J. N. Permenter (AD. August 10, 1879), Rosette Permenter (AD. August 10, 1879), M. J. Permenter (Follett, AD. August 10, 1879), S. C. Ranch (AD. August 10, 1879).

Ely-Union Valley Cumberland Presbyterian Church, Ely, Marion County, Missouri

Register of Elders

Name	Ordained	Ceased to Act
William Moss	1855	d. Feb. 20, 1886
John A. Moss	1858	Mar. 21, 1870

Name	Ordained	Ceased to Act
Darius Browning	1864	d. Mar. 17, 1879
Joseph Crim	Aug. 22, 1870	Nov. 10, 1888
John Maston	Aug. 5, 1872	Apr. 9, 1887
Wm. H. Wadsworth	May 5, 1878	---
Henry A. Potterfield	May 1, 1887	Feb. 12, 1892
Robert S. Hayden	May 1, 1887	May 29, 1899
Jos. W. Crim	Feb. 12, 1892	---
Vincent S. Corder	Aug. 13, 1899	---
Perry Maxwell	Aug. 13, 1899	---

Register of Deacons

Name	Ordained
Francis T. Wadsworth	May 1, 1887

Register of Infant Baptisms

Mary Emaline Caldwell, (PRTS) D. C. and E. R. Caldwell, (BD) December 24, 1871, (MG) James W. Devall

Henry F. Potterfield, (PRTS) H. A. and M. A. Potterfield, (BD) September 15, 1872.

Sterling E. Tuley, (PRTS) E. M. and E. L. Tuley, (BD) October 29, 1889, (MG) J. N. Lowrance.

Mable Clare Tuley, (PRTS) E. M. and E. L. Tuley, (BD) October 29, 1889, (MG) J. B. Lowrance.

Effie F. Wadsworth, (PRTS) F. T. and C. Wadsworth, (BD) August 5, 1883, (MG) J. B. Lowrance.

Clara B. Wadsworth, (PRTS) F. T. and C. Wadsworth, (BD) April 10, 1883, (MG) David Armstrong.

Mary C. Wadsworth, (PRTS) F. T. and C. Wadsworth, (BD) January 10, 1892, (MG) W. H. Jones.

Maud Luvenia Tuley, (PRTS) Elisha M. and Emma L. Tuley, (BD) January 14, 1894, (MG) W. Brooks.

Mary Lela Tuley, (PRTS) Elisha M. and Emma L. Tuley, (MG) W. Brooks.

Register of Adult Baptisms

Name	Date	Reverend
Miss Margaret F. Crim	Sep. 24, 1871	James W. Duvall
Miss Manerva Knox	Sep. 24, 1871	James W. Duvall
Edwin C. Hayden	Sep. 24, 1871	James W. Duvall
David C. Caldwell	Dec. 24, 1871	James W. Duvall
George Simpkins	Dec. 24, 1871	James W. Duvall
Mrs. Mary Roach	Nov. 5, 1876	James W. Duvall
Miss Lou Browning	Jan. 31, 1876	James W. Duvall
Mrs. Eudora Lear	Aug. 12, 1877	T. G. Pool
Miss Lulla Stephens	Sep. 2, 1877	T. G. Pool
Robert Hayden	Sep. 2, 1877	T. G. Pool
Miss Rosa E. Forman	Nov. 8, 1878	T. G. Pool
Miss Bessie Payne	Nov. 10, 1878	T. G. Pool
Miss Ella Payne	Nov. 10, 1878	T. G. Pool
Newton A. Moss	Nov. 10, 1878	T. G. Pool
Daniel F. Payne	Nov. 10, 1878	T. G. Pool

Name	Date	Reverend
John Payne	Nov. 10, 1878	T. G. Pool
Lewell H. Griffin	Nov. 10, 1878	T. G. Pool
George J. McIntye	Nov. 10, 1878	T. G. Pool
John E. Griffin	Nov. 10, 1878	T. G. Pool
John Timmons	Nov. 10, 1878	T. G. Pool
James Tuley	Nov. 10, 1878	T. G. Pool
Alexander Clark	Nov. 12, 1878	T. G. Pool
Thomas Hayden	Nov. 12, 1878	T. G. Pool
Elisha M. Tuley	Nov. 12, 1878	T. G. Pool
Charles E. Stephens	Nov. 15, 1878	T. G. Pool
Frederick Humble	Oct. 14, 1883	A. M. Buchanan
Wm. L. Edmunds	Oct. 14, 1883	A. M. Buchanan
Amos E. Ravenscroft	Oct. 14, 1883	A. M. Buchanan
Cordelia Wadsworth	Apr. 3, 1887	D. Armstrong
Theodore W. Smith	Apr. 3, 1887	D. Armstrong
Mamie Guinn	Jan. 10, 1893	H. H. Jones
Robert Corder	Jan. 10, 1893	H. H. Jones
Venie Corder	Jan. 10, 1893	H. H. Jones
J. D. Culbertson	Jan. 10, 1893	H. H. Jones
J. W. Crim	Jan. 10, 1893	H. H. Jones
Thomas Moss	Jan. 10, 1893	M. Brook
William Emery	Jan. 10, 1893	M. Brook
Annie McIntre	Jan. 10, 1893	M. Brook
Ella S. Daulton	Jul. 29, 1893	M. Brook
Miss Pearl Lear	Dec. 25, 1893	M. Brook
James H. Brooks	Feb. 11, 1894	M. Brook
James Corder	Mar. 17, 1895	M. Brook
Matilda Ellen Harris	Oct. 24, 1895	M. Brook
Isaac McIntire	Nov. 2, 1895	M. Brook
Mrs. Sarah McIntire	Nov. 2, 1895	M. Brook
Vincent S. Corder	Nov. 2, 1895	M. Brook
Willis Campbell	Nov. 2, 1895	M. Brook

Register of Marriages

John Hitch and Hester F. McCloud, (MD) April --, 1866, (MG) M. Rhodes.

H. A. Potterfield and Margaret A. Woodsworth, (MD) June 22, 1865, (MG) M. Rhodes.

J. W. Moss and --- Miload, (MD) December ---, 1866, (MG) M. Corban.

James W. Gentry and Mary D. Moss, (MD) January 2, 1866, (MG) --- Firman.

David Caldwell and Ellen R. Wadsworth, (MD) March 25, 1869, (MG) --- Faubian.

John Horn and Martha F. Moss, (MD) October 28, 1869, (MG) --- Faubian.

Joseph Hotchkiss and Naomi Dalton, (MD) September 11, 1870, (MG) John Leighton.

Saml. M. Crim and Mary D. Moss, (MD) April 6, 1869, (MG) --

— Faubian.
Wm. C. Moss and Elizabeth E. Dreshee, (MD) December 27, 1869, (MG) Mim. Bell.
Albert Dilliner and Eliza J. Wilcoxen, (MD) April 1, 1869, (MG) --- Faubian.
James W. Moss and Geneva J. Wadsworth, (MD) October 3, 1869, (MG) J. R. Taylor.
James W. Lear and Millie A. Tuley, (MD) ?, (MG) J. R. Taylor.
John W. Stephens and Harriet Payne, (MD) October 15, 1873, (MG) J. R. Taylor.
Edwin Hayden and Miss America J. Moss, (MD) October 1, 1874, (MG) J. R. Taylor.
Benjamin Walker and Miss Mary Browning, (MD) ?, (MG) J. R. Taylor.
Thomas Haiser and Miss Annie Thomas, (MD) 1874, (MG) J. R. Taylor.
Wm. Payne and Miss Emma Walker, (MD) 1874, (MG) J. R. Taylor.
Elisha M. Tuley and Miss Emma Wadsworth, (MD) December 3, 1878, (MG) T. G. Pool.
John Willis and Miss Eva Moss, (MD) February 2, 1879, (MG) T. G. Pool.
F. J. Wadsworth and Cordelia Cassady, (MD) March 30, 1880, (MG) T. G. Pool.
C. V. Hammes and Venie Potterfield, (MD) Jul. 3, 1890, (MG) T. G. Pool.
D. F. Payne and Rosa Forman, (MD) November 20, 1881, (MG) T. G. Pool.
David Payne and Lousia J. Browning, (MD) November 20, 1881, (MG) T. G. Pool.
R. L. Hayden and Maggie Crim, (MD) September 1, 1881, (MG) T. G. Pool.
Jerry Harris and Julie Frogg, (MD) February 10, 1992, (MG) --- Youngman.
John W. Crim and Abbie Mitchell, (MD) September 13, 1893, (MG) M. Brook.
Thomas Moss and Annie McIntire, (MD) November 28, 1893, (MG) M. Brook.

Register of Deaths

Name	Date
Mathew Moss	March 1, 1878
Mrs. Margaret A. Browning	April 8, 1878
Darius Browning	March 17, 1878
Mrs. Jane Moss	February 5, 1880
Mrs. Margaret Moss	February 19, 1880
Mrs. Mary A. Wadsworth	September 16, 1882
William Moss	February 20, 1896
Mrs. Abbie Crim	August 11, 1896

These persons were listed without dates: H. A. Potterfield, Bessie McIntire, Ellen R. Caldwell, Francis T. Wadsworth, J. W. Crim, Fanny Crim, Mary Crim, Mary J. Lee, Martha F. Warren, Jenuva J. Moss.

Register of Communicants

Name	Comments
William Moss	d. February 20, 1896
Mrs. Louisa Moss	Dis. November 10, 1888
Mrs. Jane Moss	d. February 5, 1880
Mrs. Mary Ann Stephens	Dis. January 8, 1883
Mathew Moss	d. March 1, 1878
Mrs. Winford Howel	d. January 6, 1888
John T. Dalton	Dis. July 17, 1871, misconduct
Mrs. Hester A. Moss	Dis. by letter
John McCloud	Dis. July 17, 1871, misconduct
Mrs. Mary E. Dalton	Dis. April 9, 1887
Miss Margaret A. Wadsworth	---
William H. Wadsworth	AD. February, 1858
William O. Forman	Removed
John A. Moss	Dis. March 21, 1870
John W. Wilcoxen	Dropped
Mrs. Eliza A. Wilcoxen	Dropped
Mary Ann Wadsworth	d. September 16, 1882
Darius Browning	d. March 17, 1879
Margaret A. Browning	d. April 8, 1878
Francis Wadsworth	---
Catharine Hayden	Dis. July 7, 1876, d. 1887
Thomas Hayden	Suspended Sep. 14, 1872
William A. Moss	Suspended
Benjamin C. Moss	Dis. February 17, 1871
Susan M. Wadsworth	---
Miss Ellen Wadsworth	---
Miss Margaret Melond	---
Mrs. Mary E. Dolton	AD. November 1, 1863, Dis. April 9, 1887
Mrs. Alice Clark	---
Mrs. Cynthia Upton	AD. January, 1869, Dis. May 17, 1874
Miss Emma Walker (Payne)	d. 1886
Miss Eliza J. Wilcoxen	d. Nov. (?) 12, 1869
William A. Williams	AD. February 28, 1865
Miss Mary D. Moss	AD. March 1, 1865, d. July 21, 1869
Hayden L. Moss	AD. March 1, 1865
Miss Sarah C. Moss	AD. March 2, 1865, Dis. September 21, 1881

Name	Comments
Mrs. Parthenia Williams	AD. March 3, 1865
Miss Martha F. Moss	AD. March 3, 1865, Dis. July 15, 1870
Mrs. Leah Richeson	AD. August 27, 1865, d. July 22, 1875
Miss Naomi Dalton	AD. August 28, 1865
Thomas Hunter	AD. September 24, 1865, d. November 5, 1870
Samuel Clark	AD. April 22, 1866, August 22, 1870
Mrs. Susan J. Horn	AD. April 22, 1866, Dis. July 10, 1870
Mrs. Elizabeth Grafford	AD. June 24, 1866
Mrs. Margaret Moss	AD. November 24, 1866, Dis. February 17, 1880
Joseph W. Crim	AD. November 24, 1866, Dis. November 10, 1888
Mrs. Leah F. Crim	AD. November 24, 1866, Dis. July 15, 1870
John Horn	AD. November 24, 1866, Dis. 1869
Mrs. Laura A. Dalton	AD. November 27, 1865
Miss Jenieva Wadsworth	AD. November 27, 1865, Dis. 1869
George Dalton	AD. November 27, 1865
Miss Mary Moss (Crim)	AD. November 27, 1865, Dis. November 10, 1888
Miss Sarah Wilcoxen	Suspended Nov. 27, 1866
William C. Moss	AD. November 27, 1866, Dis. October 15, 1873
Joseph Stephens	AD. November 27, 1866
James D. Shaw	AD. November 27, 1866, Dis. September 26, 1881
Harrison W. Moss	AD. November 27, 1866, Dis. Oct., 1872, d. 1872
Mrs. Mary Forman	AD. November 27, 1866, Joined M. E. Church
Mrs. Ann E. Howell	AD. August 23, 1868
Mrs. Elizabeth E. Moss	Dis. October 13, 1873, AD. 1870
Miss America J. Moss (Hayden)	AD. August 22, 1870, d. March 5, 1888
John Maston	AD. August 22, 1870
Miss Martha F. Wadsworth	AD. December 29, 1870
Miss Mary M. Browning	AD. August 22, 1870
Miss Mary M. Browning (Walker)	AD. August 22, 1879, Joined Christian Church
Miss Margaret F. Crim (Hayden)	AD. December 29, 1870

Name	Comments
David C. Caldwell	Ad. November 24, 1871
Miss Minerva Knox	AD. December 29, 1870, Dis. September 25, 1871
Edwin C. Hayden	AD. December 29, 1870, Dis. February 23, 1889
Miss Milliy A. Tuley (Lear)	AD. December 27, 1871
George W. Simpkins	AD. December 28, 1871
Miss Mary J. Tuley	AD. July 27, 1873
Miss Emma L. Wadsworth	AD. August 25, 1873
Miss Hattie Payne (Stephen)	AD. August 25, 1873, Dis. January 8, 1883
Miss Eva L. Moss (Willis)	AD. August 25, 1873, Dis. September 2, 1889
Miss Annie Thomas (Kiser)	AD. August 25, 1873, Suspended Nov. 10, 1897, Reinstated Aug. 26, 1898
Mistress Eudora Lear	AD. November 5, 1875
Mistress Mollie Roach	AD. November 5, 1875
Miss Lou J. Browning	AD. January 30, 1876, Dis. July 8, 1883
Henry H. Potterfield	AD. August 13, 1877, Dis. January 8, 1883
Miss Luella Stephens	AD. August 13, 1877, Dis. January 8, 1883
Robert Hayden	AD. August 13, 1877
Miss Rosa E. Forman (Payne)	AD. November 8m 1878, Dis. July 7, 1887
Miss Bessie Payne	AD. November 20, 1878, Dis. October 9, 1883
Miss Ella Payne	AD. November 10, 1878, Dis. October 9, 1883
Newton A. Moss	AD. November 10, 1878
Daniel F. Payne	AD. November 10, 1878, Dis. July 7, 1884
John Payne	AD. November 10, 1878
Lewell H. Griffin	AD. November 10, 1878, Misconduct
George J. McIntyre	AD. November 10, 1878
John E. Griffin	AD. November 10, 1878, DIs. August 21, 1882
John Timmons	AD. November 10, 1878
James Tinley	AD. November 10, 1878, Dis. February 2, 1880
Alexander Clark	AD. November 12, 1878, Dis. March 8, 1880
Thomas Hayden	AD. November 12, 1878
Elisha Tinley	AD. November 12, 1878, Dis. Apr. 12, 1880

Name	Comments
Edward Griffin	AD. April 6, 1879
Mrs. Mary Griffin	AD. April 6, 1879
Miss Vernie Potterfield	AD. December 3, 1882
Frederick Humble	AD. October 14, 1883
Wm. L. Edmunds	AD. October 14, 1883, Dis. June 8, 1885
Amos E. Ravenscraft	Ad. October 14, 1883, Suspended Apr. 9, 1887
Miss Margaretta A. Wadsworth	---
William H. Wadsworth	---
Francis Wadsworth	d. April 11, 1913
Susan M. Wadsworth	---
Miss Ellen Wadworth	d. January 9, 1912
Elizabeth Grafford	AD. June 24, 1861
Leah F. Crim	AD. November 24, 1861
Martha F. Wadsworth	AD. December 29, 1870
Margarette F. Crim	AD. December 29, 1870
David C. Caldwill	AD. December 24, 1871, d. October 25, 1903
Mary J. Tuley	AD. July 27, 1873, d. January 15, 1914
Emma L. Wadsworth	AD. August 25, 1873
Robert Hayden	AD. August 13, 1877
Edwin Griffin	AD. April 6, 1879
Mary Griffin	AD. April 6, 1879
Emma L. Potterfield	AD. December 3, 1882
Cornelia Wadsworth	AD. April 8, 1887
Annie W. Daulton	AD. April 8, 1887
Chas. E. Stephens	AD. April 8, 1887
Jacob Humble	AD. April 7, 1887, Joined the Methodists
Ida Crim	AD. January 10, 1892
Jem (sic) Harris	AD. August 5, 1890, Dis. November 15, 1910
Elisla Tuley	AD. January 10, 1892, Joined the Methodists
Mamie Crim	AD. January 10, 1892, Dis. November 5, 1910
Robert Corder	AD. January 10, 1892, Dis. December 13, 1893
Venie Corder	AD. January 10, 1892, Dis. December 13, 1893
Abbie Mitchell	AD. August 17, 1893, d. August 11, 1896
Miss Cordelia Wadsworth	AD. April 3, 1887
Theodore W. Smith	AD. April 3, 1887, Dis. November 10, 1888
Miss Annie Wakeman Daulton	AD. April 3, 1887

Name	Comments
Charles E. Stephens	AD. April 3, 1887
Mrs. Mary A. Stephens	AD. April 3, 1887, d. October 16, 1888
Mrs. Leella Smith	AD. April 3, 1887, d. October 16, 1888
Jacob Humble	AD. April 10, 1887
Miss Ida Crim	AD. October 16, 1887
Wm. L. Edmonds (d. 1888)	AD. October 16, 1887
Jerry Harris	AD. August 3, 1890
Clem Hamner	AD. September 14, 1890
Miss Mamie Crim	AD. January 10, 1892
Elisa Tuley	AD. January 10, 1892
Robert Corder	AD. January 12, 1892
Mrs. Vernie Corder	AD. January 12, 1892
Willie C. Potterfield	AD. January 10, 1892 Dis. August 13, 1894
J. D. Culbertson	AD. January 10, 1892
J. H. Crim	AD. January 10, 1892
Xenia Boulding	AD. January 10, 1892
William Emery	AD. January 10, 1892, Joined Baptists
Thomas Moss	AD. January 10, 1892
Annie McIntire	AD. January 10, 1892
Ella S. Daulton	AD. July 29, 1893, Dis. October 18, 1899
Mrs. James Lear	AD. December 13, 1898
Miss Pearl Lear	AD. December 13, 1893
Newton A. Moss	AD. December 15, 1893, Dis. January 29, 1887
James H. Brooks	AD. February 11, 1894
Miss Matilda Ellen Harris	AD. October 24, 1895
Isaac McIntyre	AD. November 2, 1895
Vincent S. Corder	AD. November 2, 1895
Miss Amelia Corder	AD. November 2, 1895
H. A. Potterfield	AD. September 15, 1896
Rev. Hiter W. James	AD. August 9, 1896
Perry Maxwell	AD. August 21, 1896
Clem Hainer	AD. September 14, 1890

The following names were listed with no dates or other information: Low. Patterson, Mrs. Patterson, Henry G. Hayden, Mrs. Hayden, Wm. Corder, Miss Stella McFortune, Delbert Lear, Homer Corder, Pearl Corder, Miss Clara Wadsworth, Lela Tuley, Miss Cleo Crim, Mrs. Mary Kiser, Jas. Wadsworth.

Mount Hope Cumberland Presbyterian Church, Huntsville, Randolph County, Missouri
Register of Marriages

P. G. Turner and Fannie E. Jenkins, (MD) May 7, 1878, (MG)

A. M. Buchanan.
Arthur (Bud) Jenkins and Mary J. Overby, (MD) September 8, 1876, (MG) T. G. Pool.

Register of Adult Baptisms

Name	Date	Reverend
Mary J. Welch	1876	Levi Haynes
Green Jenkins	Sep. 29, 1878	*S. D. Givens *(Holden, MO)
Martha E. Jenkins	Sep. 29, 1878	S. D. Givens
Lucinda P. Hoover	Sep. 29, 1878	S. D. Givens
Malinda Hoover	Sep. 29, 1878	S. D. Givens
Jacob Hoover	Apr. 18, 1890	W. F. Manning
Alfred C. Smothers	Aug. 25, 1882	J. E. Sharp
Katie Cunningham	Aug. 25, 1892	J. E. Sharp
Wm. Arthur Frazier	Aug. 31, 1882	J. E. Sharp
Isola Jenkins	Aug. 31, 1882	J. E. Sharp
Nora Jenkins	Aug. 31, 1882	J. E. Sharp
Mollie Smothers	Aug. 31, 1882	J. E. Sharp
Lisie A. Cunningham	Aug. 31, 1882	J. E. Sharp
Flora B. Wilson	Aug. 31, 1882	J. E. Sharp
Adella E. Esra	Sep. 17, 1882	J. E. Sharp
Mary A. Esry	Sep. 4, 1883	A. M. Buchanan
Warren E. Esry	Sep. 4, 1883	A. M. Buchanan
Geo. F. Brock	Sep. 5, 1883	A. M. Buchanan
Edward E. Brock	Dec. 5, 1883	A. M. Buchanan
Thomas L. Pilkerton	Dec. 5, 1883	A. M. Buchanan
Amos Weeks	Dec. 5, 1883	*J. E. Sharpe *(Reverend's name spelled two ways.)
E. Landon Heand	Dec. 5, 1883	J. E. Sharpe
Jhon (sic) Kribs	Dec. 5, 1883	J. E. Sharpe
Eva L. Jenkins	Dec. 6, 1883	J. E. Sharpe
James H. Rout	Nov. 24, 1884	James Disert
Emit H. Hardister	Nov. 24, 1884	James Disert
Cora B. Adams	Dec. 25, 1884	G. W. Baker
Mary Pilkington	Dec. 25, 1884	G. W. Baker
Mattie A. Pilkington	Dec. 25, 1884	G. W. Baker
Eugene H. Pilkington	Dec. 25, 1884	G. W. Baker
Tomie J. Owen	Dec. 25, 1884	G. W. Baker
Amanda E. Esry	Dec. 25, 1884	G. W. Baker
Lizia Miller	Dec. 25, 1884	G. W. Baker
Sinie L. Miller	Dec. 25, 1884	G. W. Baker
Jno. Wm. McCullough	Oct. 18, 1885	A. M. Buchanan
Jas. G. Alverson	Oct. 18, 1885	A. M. Buchanan
Cyrus Frazier	Oct. 18, 1885	A. M. Buchanan
Charley A. Frazier	Oct. 18, 1885	A. M. Buchanan
Ollie Harris	May 2, 1886	A. M. Buchanan
James L. McCullanah	May 2, 1886	A. M. Buchanan
Edwin J. Adams	Aug. --, 1886	A. M. Buchanan
Ida A. White	Aug. 8, 1886	A. M. Buchanan

Name	Date	Reverend
Nowel Devore	Mar. 9, 1889	H. C. Yates
Warren B. Walker	Mar. 9, 1889	H. C. Yates
Geo. Vaugh	Mar. 9, 1889	H. C. Yates
Anna Vaugh	Mar. 9, 1889	H. C. Yates
Ernest D. Adams	Mar. 9, 1889	H. C. Yates
Magie E. Jackoby	Mar. 9, 1889	H. C. Yates
Martha A. Jacoby	Mar. 9, 1889	H. C. Yates
Minnie L. Wats	Mar. 9, 1889	H. C. Yates
James C. Jenkins	Jun. 2, 1889	A. M. Buchanan
Wm. T. Chapman	Jun. 2, 1889	A. M. Buchanan
Lura Reede	Jun. 2, 1889	A. M. Buchanan
Benjamin Deskins	Mar. 2, 1890	J. L. Routt
Mrs. S. A. Deskins	Mar. 2, 1890	---
Mary J. Pilkington	Dec. 14, 1884	---
John W. Pilkington	Dec. 14, 1884	---
*Mattie A. Pilkington	Dec. 14, 1884	---

*(She claims an un-regenerate hart (sic). Her name is dropped at her own request.)

Name	Date	Reverend
Eugene H. Pilkington	Dec. 14, 1884	Dis. Mar. 8, 1893
Josmie J. Owen	Dec. 14, 1884	---
Salie (sic) B. Owen	Dec. 14, 1884	---
Amanda E. Esry	Dec. 14, 1884	Dis. Sep. 18, 1888
Lizia Miller	Dec. 14, 1884	---
Jno. Wm. McCullough	Oct. 18, 1885	Dis. Dec. 6, 1902
Jas. G. Alverson	Oct. 18, 1885	d. Mar. 6, 1910
Wm. B. Walls	Oct. 18, 1885	Dis. Mar. 17, 1888
Sarah R. Watts	Oct. 18, 1885	Dis. Mar. 17, 1888
Emil Junker	Oct. 18, 1885	Dis. Nov. 20, 1886
Cyrus Frazier	Oct. 18, 1885	Dis. Mar. 26, 1902
Charity A. Frazier	Oct. 18, 1885	---
Charles H. Ramsey	Oct. 18, 1885	---
Sarah M. Ramsey	Oct. 18, 1885	---
Rachel A. McCullough	Oct. 18, 1885	Dis. Jan. 15, 1889
Eliza Shaw	Nov. 15, 1885	Dis. Aug. 7, 1903 Joined the Mormons
Samuel P. White	Dec. 6, 1885	---
Mary C. White	Dec. 6, 1885	---
Ida A. White	Dec. 6, 1885	Dis. Jun. 2, 1892
James L. McCullough	Dec. 6, 1885	---
Isaac Harris	Feb. 8, 1886	d. Apr. 2, 1888
Ollia Harris	Feb. 17, 1886	---
Wm. Henry Tuggle	Feb. 17, 1886	Dis. Aug. 8, 1889
Edwin J. Adams	Aug. 7, 1886	Dis. Aug. 6, 1892
Gerthie L. Jenkins	Aug. 7, 1886	---
Wm. T. Chapman	Nov. 21, 1888	---
*James C. Jenkins	Nov. 21, 1888	Dis. Aug. 7, 1903

*(Went to Huntsville)

Norvel Devore	Mar. 9, 1889	---

Name	Admission	Dismissed
Warren B. Walker	Mar. 9, 1889	---
Chas. E. Miller	Mar. 9, 1889	---
Geo. Vaughn	Mar. 9, 1889	---
Anna J. Vaughn	Mar. 9, 1889	---
Robbert (sic) W. Dutten	Mar. 9, 1889	Dis. Mar. 3, 1893
Ernest D. Adams	Mar. 9, 1889	Dis. Mar. 2, 1895
Magie E. Jackoby	Mar. 9, 1889	---
Martha A. Jackoby	Mar. 9, 1889	---
Minie L. Wats	Mar. 9, 1889	Dis. Mar. 3, 1893
Tura Reede	Jun. 2, 1889	Dis. Feb. 3, 1893
Alex. M. Frazer	Aug. 12, 1889	Dis. Jul. 6, 1901
Mrs. S. A. Deskin	Feb. 2, 1809	Dis. May 19, 1899
Benjamin Deskin	Mar. 2, 1890	Dis. May 19, 1899
Alice E. Frazier	May 4, 1890	Dis. Jul. 6, 1901
Clara Walker	Oct. 5, 1890	Married W. L. Gibson
Tomie E. Sheron	Oct. 5, 1890	---
Tomie J. Esry	Oct. 5, 1890	---
Joseph A. Calvert	Nov. 30, 1890	---
L. M. Calvert	Nov. 30, 1890	d. 1891
J. W. McCullough	Nov. 30, 1890	Dis. Nov. 3, 1894
Rachel A. McCullough	Nov. 30, 1890	Dis. Nov. 3, 1894
Wm. H. Robuck	Dec. 6, 1890	d. Feb. 19, 1924
Sarah E. Robuck	Dec. 6, 1890	---
Frank White	Oct. 30, 1892	---
Bertha Deskins	Oct. 30, 1892	Dis. May 19, 1899
Barbary Breusch	Dec. 4, 1892	---
Bula Rutte	Apr. 30, 1893	---
Jacob Brush	Aug. 16, 1893	---
John C. Cox	Aug. 16, 1893	---
Geo. Morris	Aug. 7, 1895	---
Tura Morris	Aug. 7, 1895	---
Henrettie McCullough	Aug. 12, 1896	---
Laura Baker	Aug. 21, 1896	Joined the Baptists
Winnie Rais	Aug. 21, 1896	Married Robt. Harris
J. W. Baker	Aug. 21, 1896	---
Maggie Walker	Aug. 21, 1896	---
Aaron McCullough	Aug. 21, 1896	---
Edward Rais	Aug. 21, 1896	---
Thos. Gowings	Aug. 21, 1896	d. Mar. 16, 1897
Ida Gowings	Aug. 21, 1896	---
Thos. Shiflett	Aug. 21, 1896	---
Ella Shiflett	Aug. 21, 1896	---
Mrs. Bertha Shaw	Aug. 21, 1896	---
Milton F. Gooding	Aug. 21, 1896	---
Alise Shaw	Aug. 21, 1896	---
Burnard H. Shilfett	Aug. 21, 1896	---
Frank L. Baker	Aug. 21, 1896	---

Name	Admission	Dismissed
Wm. W. Shaw	Aug. 21, 1896	Joined the Mormons
Willard E. Towles	Aug. 21, 1896	Dis. Mar. 14, 1902
James C. Towles	Aug. 21, 1896	---
Selmon Harris	Aug. 21, 1896	---
David Esry	Aug. 21, 1896	---
Emma Shiflett	Aug. 21, 1896	---
Geo. T. Shiflett	Aug. 21, 1896	---
Alfred Graves	Aug. 21, 1896	Dis. Mar. 14, 1902
Lizzie Graves	Aug. 21, 1896	Dis. Mar. 14, 1902
H. R. Walker	Aug. 21, 1896	Dis. October, 1904
Belle Walker	Aug. 21, 1896	Dis. October, 1904
Lula Routte	Aug. 21, 1896	---
Thos. H. Riley	Oct. 18, 1896	---
Lydia F. Polston	Apr. 24, 1898	Dis. 1902
R. S. Polston	Aug. 7, 1898	---
Walter Shiflett	Aug. 7, 1898	Joined the church at Moberley
Wm. J. Turner	Aug. 7, 1898	---
Josafine Hosa	Aug. 12, 1898	---
Mrs. Bill Ramsey	Aug. 12, 1898	---
David G. Jones	Aug. 12, 1898	---
James Calvin Thomas	Aug. 12, 1898	---
Mrs. Nettie Thomas	Aug. 12, 1898	---
James Kidwell	Aug. 12, 1898	

Hernando Cumberland Presbyterian Church, Hernando, DeSoto County, Mississippi

Register of Elders

Name	Ordained	Ceased to Act
Milton B. Stokes	Aug. 7, 1873	---
Walter Y. Flynt	Aug. 7, 1873	---
B. F. Boulding	May 3, 1873	Aug. 15, 1874

Register of Communicants

Name	Admission	Dismissed
Mary Ann Stokes	Apr. 6, 1872	---
Mary Caroline Odom	Apr. 6, 1872	---
Ellen Jane Walker	Apr. 6, 1872	---
Kate A. Griffin	Apr. 6, 1872	---
Elizabeth M'Clarnock	Apr. 6, 1872	---
James C. Riley	Apr. 6, 1872	---
Margaret Y. Riley	Apr. 6, 1872	---
John L. Robertson	Oct. 5, 1872	Jul. 5, 1873
William H. Riley	Jul. 6, 1872	Jul. 5, 1873
Fannie Holmes Robertson	Oct. 5, 1872	Jul. 5, 1873
Emaline Robertson	Oct. 5, 1872	Jul. 5, 1873
Sanford M. Clamrock	Apr. 6, 1872	Jul. 5, 1873
Milton Byrd Stokes	Jul. 6, 1872	Jul. 5, 1873

Name	Admission	Dismissed
Walter Thornton Flynt	Jan. 6, 1873	Jul. 5, 1873
Val. Elina	Oct. 5, 1872	Jul. 5, 1873
Fannie Gillespie	Oct. 5, 1872	Jul. 5, 1873
Addie Mackey	Apr. 5, 1873	Jul. 5, 1873
Fannie Cecil Flynt	Apr. 5, 1873	Jul. 5, 1873
Ester Ann Flynt	Apr. 5, 1873	Jul. 5, 1873
Sarah J. Freeze	Jul. 5, 1873	---
Benjamin Franklin	Apr. 6, 1873	---
Mary Pullin	Aug. 7, 1873	---
Lon J. Mackey	Oct. 5, 1872	---
Robert M. Griffin	Oct. 4, 1873	Aug. 15, 1874
Lee Johnston	Oct. 4, 1873	---
Benjamin Bouldin	Jan. 3, 1874	Aug. 15, 1874
Martha Bouldin	Jan. 3, 1874	Aug. 15, 1874
Josephine Marcum	May 3, 1874	Jan. 2, 1875
Robt. E. McGarhee	Oct. 3, 1874	---
J. Lafayette Robertson	Jan. 2, 1875	---

Register of Adult Baptisms

Name	Date	Reverend
Francis Richards	Apr., 1873	B. F. Griffin
Robert E. McGarhee	Oct., 1874	B. F. Griffin
--- Marcum	Oct., 1874	B. F. Griffin
J. Lafayette Robertson	Jun., 1875	B. F. Griffin

Register of Infant Baptisms

---- Marcum (two children), (PRTS) --- Marcum and Josephine Marcum, (BD) First Sunday, October, 1875, (MG) B. F. Griffin.

Sand Spring - Mt. Pleasant Cumberland Presbyterian Church, Utica, Daviess County, Kentucky.

Register of Marriages

Jesse B. Mosley and Joanna Downess, (MD) December 19, 1837, (MG) Rev. S. Calhoun.

James P. Mosely and Julia B. Lawton, (MD) September 3, 1846, (MG) J. Wesver.

John T. Mosely and Joanna Crabtree, (MD) October 11, 1863, (MG) Rev. S. Hendrix.

Charles O. Boston and Emily H. Mosley, (MD) December 22, 1863, (MG) K. Hay.

Vircillius J. Mosley and Elizabeth J. Hatton, (MD) February 9, 1864, (MG) --- Holdman.

Mary J. Mosley and Jas. Ball, (MD) January 24, 1867, (MG) C. C. Boswell.

B. F. Collings and Ann E. Mosley, (MD) September 3, 1868

Register of Deaths
Lucy Mosley: Died April 9, 1860, age 32 y, 3 d.

Register of Communicants - Mount Pleasant

Name	Comments
Jesse B. Mosley	b. Oct., 20, 1810, MD. Dec. 19, 1837, d. Apr. 3, 1874
Joanna Mosely	b. Feb. 14, 1821
T. F. Mosely	b. Jan. 31, 1828, d. Apr. 9, 1860
*Lucy Mosley Will	b. Apr. 6, 1828, d. Whitsett 1865

*(Note: Lucy Mosley is listed with two different death dates. It is unknown if there were two women or if one of these entries is an error.)

Name	Comments
Lucy G. Atcherson	b. Apr. 17, 1821
Sarah Mosley	b. Apr. 18, 1819
Merit G. Mosely	---
Sarah E. Mosely	---
Elizabeth F. Ruby	---
Martha Oglesby	---
Dorcus Goodwin	---
John L. Goodwin	---
Vervillus L. Mosley	b. Sep. 5, 1838
James P. Mosley	b. Apr. 1, 1819
Julia B. Mosley	b. Mar. 30, 1824
Lucy Ann Smith	Dismissed without letter
Presley Lee	Dismissed without letter
John T. Mosley, Jr.	b. Sep. 5, 1840
Emily H. Mosley	b. Feb. 13, 1843, MD. Dec. 22, 1860, d. Apr. 13, 1866
David F. Lee	b. Jan. 2, 1840
John M. Lee	---
Martha E. Lee	---
Elizabeth Jackson	b. Nov. 27, 1811, Dis. Sep. 24, 1859
Susan M. Lee	---
W. W. Ruby	b. Jan. 8, 1826, Dis. Jan. 21, 1864, d. Dec. 1, 1868
Cordillard Mosley	d. Feb. 28, 1845, Bapt. Jan. 31, 1864
S. H. Johnson	---
Josephine Mosley	b. Sep. 7, 1847, Bapt. Jan. 31, 1864
Anne E. Mosley	b. May 17, 1847, Bapt. Jan. 31, 1864
Martha F. Davis	b. Jan. 16, 1845, MD. Apr. 20, 1864
Antoniette Mosley	---
Emma Moose	b. Mar. 7, 1838, MD. Dec. 25,

Name	Comments
	1869
Mary J. Mosley	b. Sep. 5, 1847, Adm. Sep. 18, 1864, Bapt. Sep. 18, 1874
Mary Ann McHoyt	Adm. Sep. 20, 1864
Eliza Jane McHoyt	Bapt. Nov. 27, 18?4, Adm. Sep. 20, 1864
Eliza Hill	Adm. Sep. 20, 1864
J. Presely Mosley	Adm. Sep. 20, 1864
Elizabeth J. Mosley	b. Aug. 24, 1846, Bapt. Sep. 24, 18?4, Adm. Sep. 24, 1864
Sallie P. Mosley	b. Aug. 5, 1851, Bapt. Nov. 24, 18?4, Adm. Sep. 24, 1864
John H. McHoyt	Bapt. Nov. 27, 18?4, Adm. Nov. 26, 1864
Jemina Gibson	Adm. Jul. 15, 1845
Luther Mosely	Bapt. Sep. 1, 18?, Adm. Sep. 1, 1846
Jane Mosley (colored)	Bapt. Sep. 1, 18?, Adm. Sep. 1, 1846
Bell V. Favers	b. May 14, 1848, Bapt. Nov. 26, 18?, Adm. Sep. 1, 1846
Lucy A. Hicks	Bapt. Nov. 26, 18?, Adm. Sep. 1, 1846
----mon Mosley (colored)	Adm. Nov. 26, 1865
Savilla Cochran	b. Oct. 7, 1811, Adm. Oct. 31, 1866
Sarah Cochran	b. Sep. 23, 1847, Bapt. Apr. 28, 18?
Fredonia Martin	Adm. Oct. 31, 1866
America Mosely	---
Ebenezer Cochran	b. Jun. 3, 1843, Bapt. Mar. 24, 18?
Rachael Baird	Gone to the Babtists (sic)
Eliza Oglesby	---
Geo. W. Davis	---
Accuba Fitts	---
Delia M. Ruby	b. Jan. 15, 1856, Adm. Aug., 1868
Cornelis Ruby	Adm. Nov. 27, 1868
Samuel P. Fitts	Adm. Nov. 27, 1868
Catherine Burns	Dismissed without letter
Thos. S. Lashbrook	Adm. Dec. 4, 1868
Thos. Hansford	---
Wm. Goodwin	Dis. Mar. 1, 1875, Bapt. Dec. 29, 18?
Wm. S. Roberts	---
F. M. Iglehart	Adm. Dec. 4, 1865
Geo. D. Kerrick	Adm. Dec. 4, 1865

Name	Comments
Margaret E. Kerrick	Adm. Dec. 4, 1865
Peter Clark	Adm. Dec. 4, 1865
Elizabeth M. Clark	Adm. Dec. 4, 1865
Lucinda Baird	Bapt. Jan. 27, 1867, Adm. Dec. 4, 1865
Sarah E. Baird	Bapt. Jan. 27, 1867, Adm. Dec. 4, 1865
Elvira J. Mosley	Adm. Dec. 4, 1865
James H. Lashbrook	Adm. Dec. 26, 1868
Amelia E. Ruby	Adm. Jan. 24, 1867
Susan Ruby	Adm. Jan. 24, 1867
James Baird	Adm. Jun. 27, 1869
Sally Mosley	Adm. Aug. 22, 1869
C. H. Patterson	---
Amanda J. Patterson	Adm. Dec. 26, 1869
Lucy A. Mosely	Bapt. Nov. 28, 1870, Adm. Nov. 28, 1870
Burrel Watkins	Bapt. Nov. 30, 1870, Adm. Nov. 30, 1870
Henry Anderson	Adm. Nov. 30, 1870
Jesse S. Stewart	Bapt. Nov. 5, 1871, Adm. Nov. 5, 1871

Register of Communicants - Sand Spring

Name	Date Received
Wm. Hansford (Elder)	Aug. 17, 1844, Old Member
John Mosely (Elder)	Aug. 17, 1844, Old Member
James Little	Aug. 17, 1844, Old Member
Wm. Little	Aug. 17, 1844, Old Member
Mary Chapman	Aug. 17, 1844, Old Member
Francis Lashbrook	Aug. 17, 1844, Old Member
Joanna Mosely	Aug. 17, 1844, Experience
Francis Crabtree	Aug. 17, 1844, Old Member
Elizabeth Crabtree	Aug. 17, 1844, Experience
Jane Little	Aug. 17, 1844, Experience
Jane Hansford	Aug. 17, 1844, Experience
Wm. Lashbrook	Aug. 17, 1844, Experience
Francis Marion Humphrey	Aug. 17, 1844, Experience
Pinckney Mosely	Aug. 17, 1844, Experience
Sarah Mosely	Aug. 17, 1844, Experience
Agnes Little	Aug. 17, 1844, Experience
Patsy Humphrey	Aug. 17, 1844, Old Member
Lucy Travis	Aug. 17, 1844, Experience
Mary Crabtree	Aug. 17, 1844, Experience
George Mark	Aug. 17, 1844, Experience
Jesse Mosely	Aug. 17, 1844, Experience
Rachel Fields	Sep. 22, 1844, Experience
--- Lanum	Sep. 22, 1844, Experience

The following names were listed without any additional

information: Darcus Goodwin, Isaac F. Moseley, Merit C. Moseley, Sarah E. Moseley, Elizabeth F. Moseley, John S. Goodwin, Hick Henderson, Vercillas L. Moseley, George H. Oglesby, Lucy Ann Smith, James P. Moseley, Julia Moseley, John T. Moseley, Jr., Presly Lee, David F. Lee, John Mat Lee, Susan H. Lee, Martha E. Little, Emily H. Moseley.

Parkes Station - Zion Cumberland Presbyterian Church, Parkes Station, Maury County, Tennessee

Register of Elders

Name	Ordained	Ceased to Act
Wm. L. Craig	Sep. 28, 1872	Nov. 8, 1880
Stephen S. Craig	Sep. 28, 1872	---
James A. Branch	Sep. 28, 1872	d.Apr. 4, 1882
John L. Cheek	---	d.Oct. 2, 1873
John Craig	Jan. 31, 1874	---
R. L. Cheek	Oct. 9, 1882	---
R. E. J. Branch	May 3, 1885	---

Register of Marriages

James A. W. Branch and Cornelia A. J. Blake, (MD) Sep. 7, 1873, (MG) T. Jeff. Dixon.

Register of Adult Baptisms

Name	Date	Reverend
Emma M. Branch	Oct. 19, 1873	J. M. Kelvey
Florence J. Cockrill	Oct. 19, 1873	J. M. Kelvey
W. W. Watson	Aug. 31, 1883	W. T. Drake
Mrs. Louisa Watson	Aug. 31, 1883	W. T. Drake
Miss M. V. Pilkenton	Aug. 31, 1883	W. T. Drake

Register of Deaths

Name	Date
H. Elizabeth Gillam	Aug. 1, 1873
John Cheek	Aug. 6, 1873
Samuel Craig	---

The following death information was listed in the church minutes:

J. A. W. Branch: d. 10 miles east of Columbia on Apr. 23, 1882, b. Jun. 13, 1849, Profused religion in 1866, Became Elder in 1872, (PP) 26, 27, (RD) Oct. 9, 1882.

Rachel Craig: b. Dec. 8, 1796, d. Aug. 26, 1883, Joined the church at age 15, member for 72 y, (PP) 29, 30, (RD) Nov. 10, 1883.

Martha M. Box: daughter of Frances Box, b. Jul. 28, 1824, d. Feb. 27, 1885 at age: 60 y, 6 m, 29 d, (PP) 34, 35, (RD) May 2, 1885.

J. L. Cheek: d. Oct. 2, 1873, Maury Co., age: 72 y, 1 d, (PP) 9, (RD) Apr. 4, 1874.

Register of Communicants

Name	Comments
Samuel Miles	Dis. Sep. 6, 1874

Name	Comments
Mary L. Murphey	Dis. Sep. 14, 1877, Expelled
Nancy J. Park	Dis. Jul. 6, 1878
M. J. Uzzell	Dis. Nov. 22, 1880
M. A. E. Branch	---
John L. Cheek	Adm. Mar. 15, 1873, Dis. By Death Oct. 2, 1873
Emma M. Branch	Adm. Oct. 7, 1873
Florence J. Cockrill	Adm. Oct. 19, 1873
Samuel Miles	Adm. Jun. 20, 1875, Dis. Mar. 5, 1076
J. Aren Cheek	Adm. Sep. 19, 1876
Frances Smith	Adm. May 20, 1877
Samuel Craig	Adm. Sep. 9, 1879
Mattie M. Branch	Adm. Sep. 18, 1879, Dis. Sep. 12, 1881
Mattie E. Craig	Adm. Nov. 26, 1879, Dis. Nov. 8, 1880.
N. E. Craig	Marked Through
L. B. Craig	Adm. Nov. 26, 1879
C. E. Uzzell	Adm. Nov. 26, 1879, Dis. Nov. 22, 1880
Seth M. Branch	Adm. Nov. 26, 1879, Dis. Nov. 22, 1880
M. E. O. Branch	Adm. Nov. 26, 1879, Dis. Sep. 21, 1893
C. E. Watson	Adm. Nov. 26, 1879, Dis. Sep. 10, 1887
R. S. D. Rook	Adm. Aug. 29, 1880
A. C. E. Cheek	Adm. Oct. 6, 1880, Joined the Methodists
W. B. Rook	Adm. Oct. 6, 1880, Dis. Oct. 1, 1887
M. A. Uzzell	Adm. Oct. 6, 1880, Dis. Nov. 22, 1880
L. R. Craig	Adm. Oct. 6, 1880
Caroline Patrie	Adm. Oct. 12, 1882, Deaf & Dumb
Susan E. Cheek	Adm. Oct. 12, 1882, d. Aug. 6, 1887
Marthies J. J. Cheek	Adm. Oct. 12, 1882
Nanie B. Branch	Adm. Oct. 12, 1882, Dis. Oct. 6, 1893
W. W. Watson	Adm. Aug. 31, 1883
Louisa Watson	Adm. Aug. 31, 1883
M. N. Pilkinton	Adm. Aug. 31, 1883
M. M. Branch	Adm. Jul. 25, 1884
Matilda Hambrick	Adm. May 3, 1885, Dis. Oct. 20, 1886

Name	Comments
J. A. W. Watson	Adm. Sep. --, 1887

Alred-Shiloh Cumberland Presbyterian Church, Shiloh, Overton County, Tennessee

Register of Elders

Name	Ordained	Ceased to Act
A. C. Cooper	---	d. Jan. 20, 1885
Troy Vaughan	Aug. 11, 1871	Jan. 27, 1880
J. C. L. French	---	d. Aug. 27, 1931
H. P. Boswell	Aug. 21, 1878	Oct. 5, 1905
*Andrew Boswell	Sep. 11, 1882	d. May 8, 1888
*(Killed by a falling tree)		
*Alford Cantrell	Aug. 16, 1889	May 5, 1913
*(Killed by a falling tree)		
E. J. Stout	Sep. 8, 1889	1911
S. A. Dishman	Sep. 9, 1894	---

Register of Deaths

Name	Death Date	Remarks
L. C. Matheny	Jul. 20, 1880	Pastor
Polly Brown	Jun. 19, 1881	---
Margaret M. Poster	Aug. 8, 1883	
A. C. Looper	Jun. 20, 1885	Church Elder
Frida French	Apr. 30, 1883	
Andrew J. Boswell	May 8, 1888	Church Elder
Ruhamey Stout	Jun. 25, 1892	
Hanna Sout	Nov. 10, 1892	
Fanna Allred	Dec, 25, 1892	
J. A. Cantrel	Jul. 13, 1893	
A. O. Smith	Feb. 23, 1894	Daughter of W. C. Cantrell
Matilda Davis	May 1, 1894	
N. E. Allred	Jun. 6, 1894	
L. T. Ledbeter	Jun. 13, 1894	
M. L. Ledbeter	Oct. 13, 1894	
R. P. E. Stout	Jul. 20, 1895	
B. F. Allred	Jul. 9, 1896	
Clerisa Boswell	Mar. 16, 1898	
Leonard Stout	May 25, 1898	
S. H. Looper	Jul. 17, 1898	
M. L. French	Nov. 11, 1898	
John S. Martain	Apr. 21, 1904	
D. B. Cantrell	Apr. 27, 1905	
R. P. Looper	Sep. 29, 1904	
Mary Austen	Apr. 21, 1908	
I. M. Stout	Aug. 27, 1908	

Register of Infant Baptisms

J. B. French, (PRTS) J. C. L. French, (BD) 1880, (MG) S. K. Fillips.

A. A. French, (PRTS) J. C. L. French, (BD) 1880, (MG) S. K. Fillips.
T. W. French, (PRTS) J. C. L. French, (BD) 1880, (MG) S. K. Fillips.
G. T. French, (PRTS) J. C. L. French, (BD) 1883, (MG) Stephen Davis.
V. M. French, (PRTS) J. C. L. French, (BD) 1890, (MG) Stephen Davis.
Juda French, (PRTS) J. C. L. French, (BD) 1890, (MG) Stephen Davis.
J. C. L. Hill, (PRTS) L. M. Hill, (BD) 1890, (MG) Stephen Davis.
I. C. D. Hill, (PRTS) L. M. Hill, (BD) Nov. 29, 1891, (MG) Stephen Davis.
Abbety (?) French, (PRTS) J. C. L. French, (BD) Jun. 23, 1907, (MG) R. W. Moss.
Cytha French, (PRTS) J. C. L. French, (BD) Jun. 23, 1907, (MG) R. W. Moss.
Cleto Hill, (PRTS) Leona Hill, (BD) Aug. 15, 1907, (MG) R. W. Moss.
Myrtle Hill, (PRTS) Leona Hill, (BD) Apr. 25, 1909, (MG) W. C. Cantrell.
Olie M. E. Hill, (PRTS) Leona Hill, (BD) Apr. 14, 1912. (MG) J. E. Huffines.

Register of Adult Baptisms

Name	Date	Reverend
Matilda L. Cantrell	Apr. 18, 1880	L. C. Mutheny
Alice Carr	Oct. 1, 1880	*S. K. Fillips
John S. Martain	Mar. 13, 1881	*S. K. Philiips

*(Reverend S. K. Phillips or S. K. Fillips is spelled both ways in the record.)

Name	Date	Reverend
Mary Allred	Aug. 19, 1881	S. K. Phillips
Sary Allfred	Aug. 19, 1881	S. K. Phillips
Foster Parret	Aug. 19, 1881	S. K. Phillips
Jesa Ledbetter	Aug. 19, 1881	S. K. Phillips
Margaret Ledbetter	Aug. 19, 1881	S. K. Phillips
M. A. Vaughn	Aug. 19, 1881	S. K. Phillips
T. Q. Cantrell	Aug. 19, 1881	S. K. Phillips
J. C. Ledbetter	Aug. 19, 1881	S. K. Phillips
Parsaelia Stout	Sep. 15, 1882	S. K. Phillips
S. E. Boswell	Sep. 15, 1882	S. K. Phillips
William Allred	Sep. --, 1884	S. K. Phillips
B. J. Allred	Sep. --, 1884	S. K. Phillips
Loneler (sic) Carr	Aug. 4, 1885	J. M. Martain
Fanna Belle Carr	Aug. 4, 1885	J. M. Martain
W. C. Cook	Aug. 4, 1885	J. M. Martain
Asinn Allread (sic)	Aug. 4, 1885	J. M. Martain
Dana Smith	Aug. 4, 1885	J. M. Martain
Amanda Cook	Aug. 4, 1885	J. M. Martain

Name	Date	Reverend
Ayrilla Cantrell	Aug. 4, 1885	J. M. Martain
Abllar (sic) Cook	Aug. 3, 1885	J. M. Martain
Flourida Cook	Aug. 3, 1885	J. M. Martain
Helen Cantrell	Oct. 10, 1885	W. C. Cantrell
W. J. Cantrell	Oct. 10, 1885	W. C. Cantrell
S. E. Ledbetter	Oct. 30, 1888	W. C. Cantrell
Jane Bilbrey	Oct. 30, 1888	W. C. Cantrell
Susan Cantrell	Oct. 30, 1888	W. C. Cantrell
W. P. Stout	Oct. 30, 1888	W. C. Cantrell
M. R. Stout	Oct. 30, 1888	W. C. Cantrell
G. D. Ledbeter	Oct. 30, 1888	W. C. Cantrell
J. A. Smith	Oct. 30, 1888	W. C. Cantrell
L. M. Hill	Oct. 30, 1888	W. C. Cantrell
A. P. Ledbeter	Oct. 30, 1888	W. C. Cantrell
Mildey Crage (sic)	Oct. 30, 1888	W. C. Cantrell
N. E. Ledbetter	Oct. 30, 1888	W. C. Cantrell
J. P. Ledbetter	Oct. 30, 1888	W. C. Cantrell
Tildy Tinch	Oct. 30, 1888	W. C. Cantrell
S. A. Tinch	Oct. 30, 1888	W. C. Cantrell
Rachel Tinch	Oct. 30, 1888	W. C. Cantrell
B. F. Allred	Oct. 30, 1888	W. C. Cantrell
F. E. Allred	Oct. 30, 1888	W. C. Cantrell
J. L. Allred	Oct. 30, 1888	W. C. Cantrell
M. L. Fench	Nov. 9, 1880	Stephen Davis
S. A. Dishmon	Aug. 12, 1891	J. W. Copland
M. L. Dishmon	Aug. 12, 1891	J. W. Copland
Winna Allred	Aug. 13, 1891	W. C. Cantrell
I. D. Boswell	Aug. 13, 1891	W. C. Cantrell
Leanard Stout	Aug. 13, 1891	W. C. Cantrell
A. P. Allred	Sep. 13, 1891	W. C. Cantrell
A. Y. Boswell	Sep. 13, 1891	J. W. Copland
Mary Oston	Oct. 10, 1885	W. C. Cantrell
Louisa Miller Oston	Aug. 10, 1886	W. C. Cantrell
Mary Ana Oston	Aug. 10, 1886	W. C. Cantrell
Mary Elen Cantrell (sic)	Aug. 15, 1888	W. C. Cantrell
Candes Ramsey	Aug. 15, 1888	W. C. Cantrell
Elender Jane Cantrell	Sep. 9, 1888	W. C. Cantrell
Fanna Allred	Sep. 9, 1888	W. C. Cantrell
Alford Cantrell	Sep. 9, 1888	W. C. Cantrell
Jimey Allred	Sep. 9, 1888	W. C. Cantrell
R. A. Cantrell	Aug. 16, 1889	W. C. Cantrell
J. W. Cantrell	Aug. 16, 1889	W. C. Cantrell
C. C. Bilbrey	Aug. 16, 1889	W. C. Cantrell
T. G. Grider	Aug. 16, 1889	W. C. Cantrell
P. B. Bilbrey	Aug. --, 1889	W. C. Cantrell
M. L. Bilbrey	Aug. --, 1889	W. C. Cantrell
C. A. Stout	Aug. --, 1889	W. C. Cantrell
J. V. Cantrell	Aug. --, 1889	W. C. Cantrell

Name	Date	Reverend
F. A. Cantrell	Aug. --, 1889	W. C. Cantrell
J. H. Boman	Sep. --, 1889	Stephen Davis
Eda Hammock	Sep. --, 1889	Stephen Davis
S. J. Allred	Sep. --, 1889	W. C. Cantrell
? P. Cantrell	Sep. --, 1889	W. C. Cantrell
M. A. M. Vaughn	Sep. --, 1889	W. C. Cantrell
F. F. B. Stout	Oct. 30, 1889	W. C. Cantrell
S. G. Dishmon	Oct. 30, 1889	W. C. Cantrell
M. L. Boman	Dec. 9, 1891	W. C. Cantrell
Ruhamey Stout	Apr. 17, 1892	W. C. Cantrell
S. M. Looper	Jul. 31, 1892	W. C. Cantrell
M. A. Allred	Jul. 31, 1892	W. C. Cantrell
W. K. P. Ledbeter	Aug. 9, 1892	W. C. Cantrell
Jim Alred	Sep. 9, 1900	W. C. Cantrell
Porter Johnson	Sep. 9, 1900	W. C. Cantrell
Verna Looper	Sep. 9, 1900	W. C. Cantrell
Addie Lee Looper	Sep. 9, 1900	W. C. Cantrell
Lener Boswell	Sep. 9, 1900	W. C. Cantrell
Maryan Elred (sic)	Jun. 23, 1907	R. W. Moss
Malisse French	Jun. 23, 1907	R. W. Moss
Lona Cantrell	Jun. 23, 1907	R. W. Moss
Etty Ramsey	Jun. 23, 1907	R. W. Moss
Winna Cantrell	Jun. 23, 1907	R. W. Moss
Nora Cantrell	Jun. 23, 1907	R. W. Moss
Birthay (sic) Ramsey	Jun. 23, 1907	R. W. Moss
Nervy Dishman	Jun. 23, 1907	R. W. Moss
M. C. Bilbrey	Jun. 23, 1907	R. W. Moss
Morneyglee (sic) French	Jun. 23, 1907	R. W. Moss
Juda French	Aug. 15, 1907	R. W. Moss
Mahala Stout	Aug. 15, 1907	R. W. Moss
Elbert Stout	Aug. 15, 1907	R. W. Moss
Leona Hill	Aug. 15, 1907	R. W. Moss

Register of Communicants

Name	Comments
W. C. Cantrel	Adm. 1854, d. Nov. 19, 1911
J. A. Cantrel	Adm. 1854, d. Jun., 1893
Tray Vaughn	Adm. 1854, Dis. Jul. 17, 1880
Nancy R. Vaughn	Adm. 1854, Dis. Jul. 17, 1880
I. B. Bilberry	Adm. 1854, d. Aug. 2, 1929, Age: 79 y, 2 m, 5 d
I. M. Stout	Adm. 1854, d. Aug. 27, 1908
Winney Stout	Adm. 1854
Mary B. Cantrel	Adm. 1854, d. Nov. 26, 1917, Age: 81 y, 7 m, 1 d
Judy A. Stout	Adm. 1854, d. Feb. 10, 1913, Near 3 am.
N. P. French	Adm. 1845
Rebecca C. French	Adm. 1845

Name	Comments
M. M. French	Adm. 1845
Judy French	Adm. 1845
M. J. French	Adm. 1845
Sarrah Biberry	Adm. 1845, d. Mar. 21, 1914, Age: 81 y, 1 m 15 d
Nicy Looper	Adm. Oct. 12, 1845
Agga Walker	---
I. E. C. French	d. Aug. 27, 1931
W. T. R. Alred	---
W. H. Bilbery	d. Feb. 4, 1924
Polly Tee	---
Matilda Looper	---
A. C. Looper	---
Magness Looper	Dis. Oct., 1877
Pollieanna Looper	Dis. Oct., 1877
D. B. Cantrill (sic)	---
Nancy Cantrill (sic)	---
Cintha Copeland	---
M. A. Ledbetter	d. Dec. 16, 1894
Clerisa Boswell	d. Mar. 16, 1898, wife of Andrew Boswell
M. E. Boswell	Dis. Jul. 27, 1880
Martha M. Ramsey	b. Jun. 19, 1857, d. Sep. 16, 1950, Age: 93 y, Buried Falling Springs
R. P. T. Cantrill	Adm. Aug., 1877
M. A. M. Ramsey or Vaughn	Adm. Aug. 1877, Dis. Jul. 27, 1885
R. P. Ramsey	---
Nancy Speck	---
I. H. Looper	---
Laisa (sic) Stout	---
Elisabeth Boman	d. Sep. 11, 1919
Polly Brown	d. Jun. 18, 1881
E. J. Stout	Adm. Jul., 1878, Dis. Jan. 2, 1916
L. J. Coplan (sic)	Adm. Aug., 1878
M. E. Linder	Adm. Aug., 1878, Dis. Sep. 11, 1915, Moved to Okla. Oct. 5, 1905
H. P. Boswell	Adm. Aug., 1878
J. W. Smith	Adm. Aug., 1878
Mary Smith	Adm. Aug., 1878
O. T. Smith	Adm. Aug., 1878
Vestine Bilbery	Adm. Aug., 1878
Finey Bilbrey	Adm. Aug., 1878, d. January
Abrem (sic) Vaughn	Adm. Aug., 1878, Dis. Oct. 7, 1880, d. 1931
Mary L. Stout	Adm. Aug., 1878

Name	Comments
Lonita Carr	Adm. Aug. 4, 1885, Dis. Nov. 9, 1885
Fana Billy Carr	Adm. Aug. 4, 1885, Dis. Nov. 9, 1885
W. C. Cook	Adm. Aug. 4, 1885, Dis. Nov. 9, 1885
Asina Allread	Adm. Aug. 4, 1885
Dana Smith	Adm. Aug. 4, 1885, Dis. Apr. 20, 1895, Renewed Aug., 1921
Amanda Cook	Adm. Aug. 4, 1885, Dis. Jun. 14, 1889
Aquilla Cantrell	Adm. Aug. 4, 1885, d. Feb. 23, 1894, wife of Ben Smith
Arabella Cook	Adm. Aug. 5, 1885, Dis. Jun. 14, 1887
Flourida Cook	Adm. Aug. 5, 1885, Dis. Feb. 16, 1888
Helen Cantrell	Adm. Oct. 10, 1885
W. J. Cantrell	Adm. Oct. 10, 1885, d. Oct. 19, 1912
Mary Oston	Adm. Oct. 10, 1885, d. Apr. 21, 1908
Louisa Miller (Osten)	Adm. Aug. 10, 1886
Mary Dena Ostin	Adm. Aug. 10, 1886
Nancy Elen Cantrell(sic)	Adm. Aug. 15, 1888, d. Jun. 6, 1894, wife of B. F. Allred
Cansler (sic) Ramsey	Adm. Aug. 15, 1888, d. Mar. 22, 1928, Cause of death: paralices
Elender Jane Cantrell	Adm. Sep. 9, 1888
Fanna Allred	Adm. Sep. 9, 1888
Alford Cantrell	Adm. Sep. 9, 1888, d. May 2, 1913, Killed by a tree instantly
Jimey Allred	Adm. Sep. 9, 1888, d. Nov. 10, 1926
R. A. Cantrell	Adm. Aug. 16, 1889
J. W. Cantrell	Adm. Aug. 16, 1889, Dis. May 14, 1893
C. C. Bilbary	Adm. Aug. 16, 1889, d. Apr. 14, 1893
Y. G. Grider	Adm. Aug. 16, 1889
M. A. Grider	Adm. Aug. 16, 1889
P. B. Bilary	Adm. Aug. 1889, d. Mar. 31, 1909, wife of T. D. Cantrell
M. L. Bilbary	Adm. Aug. 1889
C. A. Stout	Adm. Aug. 1889, d. Aug. 5, 1910, in Arkansas
J. V. Cantrell	Adm. Aug. 1889
F. A. Cantrell	Adm. Aug. 1889

Name	Comments
J. A. Boman	Adm. Aug. 1889, Dis. Apr. 20, 1895
J. D. Cantrill (sic)	Adm. Aug. 1889
Eda Hammock	Adm. Aug. 1889, d. Sep. 1, 1913
S. J. Allred	Adm. Aug. 1889, d. Jul. 9, 1928
M. P. Cantrell	Adm. 1889
M. A. M. Vaughn	---
T. F. B. Stout	---
Josia Stout	d. Jun. 6, 1949
S. E. Ledbetter	Adm. Oct. 30, 1889
Jane Bilbrey (sic)	Adm. Oct. 30, 1889, d. Jul. 2, 1933, Age: 84 y, 11 m, 26 d
Susan Bilbrey (sic)	Adm. Oct. 30, 1889, d. Apr. 18, 1920
Pate (sic) Stout	Adm. Oct. 30, 1889
G. U. Ledbetter	Adm. Oct. 30, 1889, Dis. Mar. 12, 1893
J. A. Smith	Adm. Oct. 30, 1889
L. M. Hill	Adm. Oct. 30, 1889
Alto Ledbetter	Adm. Oct. 30, 1889
Milda Cray	Adm. Oct. 30, 1889
N. E. Ledbetter	Adm. Oct. 30, 1889
J. P. Ledbetter	Adm. Oct. 30, 1889
Tilily (sic) Tinch	Adm. Oct. 30, 1889
A. C. Tinch	Adm. Oct. 30, 1889, Dis. Aug. 28, 1912
Rachel Tinch	Adm. Oct. 30, 1889, Dis. Aug. 28, 1912
B. F. Allred	Adm. Sep. 17, 1880, d. Dec. 13, 1936 (maybe)
F. E. Allred	Adm. Sep. 17, 1880
J. L. Allred	Adm. Sep. 17, 1880, d. Jun. 9, 1876, Age: 77 y
M. L. French	Adm. Nov. 9, 1890, d. Nov. 11, 1898
S. A. Dishmon	Adm. Aug. 12, 1891
I. D. Boswell	Adm. Aug. 13, 1891
Winna Allred	Adm. Aug. 13, 1891, d. Oct. 27, 1927
Lenard Stout	Adm. Aug. 13, 1891
A. P. Allred	Adm. Sep. 13, 1891, Dis. 1924
A. Z. Boswell	Adm. Sep. 13, 1891
S. G. Dishmon	Adm. Sep. 13, 1891, Dis. Apr. 20, 1895
M. L. Boman	Adm. Dec. 9, 1891, d. Feb. 15, 1911
Ruhamey (sic) Stout	Adm. Apr. 17, 1892, d. Jun. 25, 1892

Name	Comments
S. M. Looper	Adm. Jul. 31, 1892
M. A. Allred	Adm. Jul. 31, 1892
W. K. P. Ledbeter	Adm. Aug. 19, 1892, Dis. Dec. 16, 1911
Jim Alred	Adm. Sep. 9, 1900
Porter Jhonson (sic)	Adm. Sep. 9, 1900
Verna Looper	Adm. Sep. 9, 1900
Adadasee Looper	Adm. Sep. 9, 1900
Lener Boswell	Adm. Sep. 9, 1900
Maryan Eldreg (sic)	Adm. Jun. 23, 1907
Malisse French	Adm. Jun. 23, 1907

Watson Cumberland Presbyterian Church, Watson, Atchison County, Missouri

Register of Elders

Name	Ordained	Ceased to Act
Wm. L. Reeves	Feb., 1867	Feb., 1884
Jesse M. Cross	Feb., 1867	d. Jan. 1, 1871
Isaac B. Jones	---	---
David McNeal	---	Feb., 1884
W. M. R. Dean	Jun., 1876	---
Daniel B. Morgan	Feb., 1867	---
Thomas McAlravy	Feb., 1867	---
Whitley McNeal	Feb., 1867	---
Adam C. Good	Feb., 1867	---
Salrid Addington (sic)	Dec., 1877	---
A. S. Campbell	Mar. 22, 1878	---
M. M. Good	Mar. 14, 1886	---
Sylvester Hall	Mar. 14, 1886	---

Register of Deacons

Name	Ordained
David McNeal	Feb., 1867
Robert Furgeson	Feb., 1867
H. J. Good	Jan., 1871
Henry Barnhart	Jan., 1871
A. S. Campbell	Jan., 1871
John Garst	May, 1876
Manon Good	Mar. 22, 1878
Willie Good	Mar. 14, 1886
June Campbell	Mar. 14, 1886
John Garst, Jr.	Dec. 14, 1888

Register of Adult Baptisms

Name	Date	Reverend
Jackson M. Brown	Feb., 1876	T. K. Roach
Martha Clodfelter	Feb., 1876	T. K. Roach
Sarah Hays	Feb., 1876	T. K. Roach
Elizabeth Good	Feb., 1876	T. K. Roach
Jammie C. McNeal	Feb., 1876	T. K. Roach

Name	Date	Reverend
Mary E. McNeal	Feb., 1876	T. K. Roach
Permelia J. Turner	Feb., 1876	T. K. Roach
Lowley Martin	Feb., 1876	T. K. Roach
Laura M. Morgan	Feb., 1876	T. K. Roach
Landon W. Campbell	Feb., 1876	T. K. Roach
Eddie F. Reeves	Feb., 1876	T. K. Roach
David J. McNeal	Feb., 1876	T. K. Roach
Abraham Bowman	Feb., 1876	T. K. Roach
John T. Clodfelter	Feb., 1876	T. K. Roach
Lafayette Morgan	Feb., 1876	T. K. Roach
Louisa J. Morgan	Feb., 1876	T. K. Roach
Anna Workman	Feb., 1876	T. K. Roach
Edmonia Barnhart	Feb., 1876	T. K. Roach
Thos. Wm. McIlravz	Feb., 1876	T. K. Roach
John L. McIlravz	Feb., 1876	T. K. Roach
Chas. R. Bushon	Feb., 1876	T. K. Roach
John H. Vanderslice	Feb., 1876	T. K. Roach
Daniel Vanderslice	Feb., 1876	T. K. Roach
Claib. J. Barnhart	Feb., 1876	T. K. Roach
John E. Davis	Feb., 1876	T. K. Roach
Mildred E. Rhodes	Feb., 1876	T. K. Roach
Catharine Harris	Feb., 1876	T. K. Roach
William H. Morgan	Feb., 1876	T. K. Roach
Alexander McLoed	Feb., 1876	T. K. Roach
Valentine Johnson	Feb., 1876	T. K. Roach
Henry R. Hales	Feb., 1876	T. K. Roach
Thomas Hays	Feb., 1876	T. K. Roach
W. L. Johnson	Feb., 1876	T. K. Roach
Wm. R. C. Clark	Nov. 15, 1878	J. C. Moore
Chas. W. Goodwin	Nov. 15, 1878	J. C. Moore
Burrell L. Goodwin	Dec. 10, 1878	J. C. Moore
John E. Smith	Dec. 10, 1878	J. C. Moore
John J. Hughes	Dec. 10, 1878	J. C. Moore
Joseph B. Goodwin	Dec. 10, 1878	J. C. Moore
Mary J. Reeves	Dec. 10, 1878	J. C. Moore
Flora E. Winkle	Dec. 10, 1878	J. C. Moore
Caroline King	Dec. 10, 1878	J. C. Moore
Leora A. Clark	Nov. 15, 1878	J. C. Moore
Mary M. Goodwin	Nov. 15, 1878	J. C. Moore
Margaret Goodwin	Nov. 15, 1878	J. C. Moore
Mary E. Brown	Nov. 15, 1878	J. C. Moore
Hannah L. Reeves	Nov. 15, 1878	J. C. Moore
Mary McFarland	Nov. 15, 1878	J. C. Moore
Sarah Hannan	1870	O. D. Allen
Elisha R. Wood	Jan. 26, 1879	J. C. Moore
Nettie E. Peacock	Jan. 26, 1879	J. C. Moore
Sarah E. Goodwin	Jan. 26, 1879	J. C. Moore
Wm. J. Goodwin	Jan. 26, 1879	J. C. Moore

Name	Date	Reverend
John J. Hughes	Dec. 10, 1878	J. C. Moore
Joseph B. Goodwin	Dec. 10, 1878	J. C. Moore
Mary J. Reeves	Dec. 10, 1878	J. C. Moore
Flora E. Winkle	Dec. 10, 1878	J. C. Moore
Caroline King	Dec. 10, 1878	J. C. Moore
Leora A. Clark	Nov. 15, 1878	J. C. Moore
Mary M. Goodwin	Nov. 15, 1878	J. C. Moore
Margaret Goodwin	Nov. 15, 1878	J. C. Moore
Mary E. Brown	Nov. 15, 1878	J. C. Moore
Hannah L. Reeves	Nov. 15, 1878	J. C. Moore
Mary McFarland	Nov. 15, 1878	J. C. Moore
Sarah Hannan	1870	O. D. Allen
Elisha R. Wood	Jan. 26, 1879	J. C. Moore
Nettie E. Peacock	Jan. 26, 1879	J. C. Moore
Sarah E. Goodwin	Jan. 26, 1879	J. C. Moore
Wm. J. Goodwin	Jan. 26, 1879	J. C. Moore
James M'Million	Jan. 26, 1879	J. C. Moore
Mary M'Million	Jan. 26, 1879	J. C. Moore
Salina C. Dunwoody	Feb., 1879	J. C. Moore
Mary E. Stifle	Feb., 1879	J. C. Moore
Dora Eastridge	Feb., 1879	J. C. Moore
Jacob Stephens	Feb., 1879	J. C. Moore
Nathan F. Hays	Feb., 1879	J. C. Moore
Andrew J. Ruble	Feb., 1879	J. C. Moore
James L. Craig	Jun., 1879	J. C. Moore
John E. Ruble	Jun., 1879	J. C. Moore
John H. Hays	Jun., 1879	J. C. Moore
Annie E. Hays	Jun., 1879	J. C. Moore
Carrie B. Warfield	Feb., 1880	J. C. Moore
Mary E. Campbell	Feb., 1880	J. C. Moore
Ada B. Peacock	Feb., 1880	J. C. Moore
Lorna J. Dunham	Feb., 1880	J. C. Moore
J. Russell McNeal	Jan., 1881	J. C. Moore
Jacob N. Campbell	Jan., 1881	J. C. Moore
Alice E. Sterritt	Jan., 1881	J. C. Moore
Adaline Browning	Jan., 1881	J. C. Moore
Dora Noble	Jan., 1881	J. C. Moore
Flora B. Rhodes	Jan., 1881	J. C. Moore
Ida F. Warfield	Jan., 1881	J. C. Moore
Emma B. Geele	Jan., 1881	J. C. Moore
Miriam Hannon	Apr., 1881	J. C. Moore
James H. Browning	May, 1881	J. C. Moore
M. A. Browning	May, 1881	J. C. Moore
Alice Thornhill	Jan., 1882	J. C. Moore
Sarah M. Addington	Jan., 1882	J. C. Moore
Henry A. Shandy	Dec., 1882	J. C. Moore
Dora A. Barnhart	Dec., 1882	J. C. Moore
Minnie D. Sliger	Dec., 1882	J. C. Moore

Name	Date	Reverend
Elizabeth C. Hall	Dec., 1882	J. C. Moore
Mincie A. Hughs	Dec., 1882	J. C. Moore
Mary A. Hall	Dec., 1882	J. C. Moore
Elizabeth J. Brown	Dec., 1882	J. C. Moore
William E. Shandy	Dec., 1882	J. C. Moore
William H. Eddington	Dec., 1882	J. C. Moore
Jacob C. Shandy	Dec., 1882	J. C. Moore
Jasper M. Hughs	Dec., 1882	J. C. Moore
Alice J. Shandy	Dec., 1882	J. C. Moore
Wm. H. Eastridge	Jan., 1883	Rev. Hodges
Alonzo A. Watts	Jan., 1883	Rev. Hodges
Lee R. Horn	Jan., 1883	Rev. Hodges
Wm. H. Good	Jan., 1883	Rev. Hodges
John H. Hudson	Jan., 1883	Rev. Hodges
Charles M. Hale	Jan., 1883	Rev. Hodges
Geo. H. Morgan	Jan., 1883	Rev. Hodges
Ellenora Nix	Mar., 1883	J. C. Moore
Mary E. Hays	Jan., 1884	J. C. Moore
Chas. Pickett	Jan., 1884	J. C. Moore
Ada M. Noels	Feb., 1884	J. C. Moore
Ritha Hall	Jan., 1884	J. C. Moore
John B. Garst	Jul., 1884	J. C. Moore
William Garst	Jul., 1884	J. C. Moore
Nellie J. Goose	Feb., 1885	J. C. Moore
Mary E. Harrison	Dec., 1885	J. C. Moore
Seletha J. Morrow	Dec., 1885	J. C. Moore
Josephine Garst	Dec., 1885	J. C. Moore
Winford H. Morgan	Dec., 1885	J. C. Moore
Hannah E. Hay	Dec., 1885	J. C. Moore
Oscar York	Dec., 1885	J. C. Moore
Jesse O. Garst	Dec., 1885	J. C. Moore
Brookens Campbell	Dec., 1885	J. C. Moore
Oliver York	Dec., 1885	J. C. Moore
Minnie Good	Aug., 1887	J. H. Tharp
Nettie Hays	Aug., 1887	J. H. Tharp
Lillie Lane	Jan., 1888	Geo. W. Hawley
Susan Lane	Jan., 1888	Geo. W. Hawley
Mary C. Hays	Jan., 1888	Geo. W. Hawley
Alice Herron	Jan., 1888	Geo. W. Hawley
Chas. Buck	Jan., 1888	Geo. W. Hawley
Noah Lane	Jan., 1888	Geo. W. Hawley
Oran Garst	Dec., 1888	(sic)C. W. Powers
Effie Garst	Dec., 1888	C. W. Powers
Josie Dirnel	Dec., 1888	C. W. Powers
Charlotta Noble	Dec., 1888	(sic)C. B. Powers
Hugh L. Hays	Dec., 1888	C. B. Powers
Peter Newman	Dec., 1888	C. B. Powers
H. Newman	Dec., 1888	C. B. Powers

Name	Date	Reverend
H. Fosket	Dec., 1888	C. B. Powers
May E. Matherly	Dec., 1888	C. B. Powers
Lillian Lutz	Dec., 1888	C. B. Powers
John Furgeson	Dec., 1888	C. B. Powers
Lulie B. Hay	Aug., 1890	C. B. Powers
Minnie Burns	Aug., 1890	C. B. Powers
Charles Unicore	Aug., 1890	C. B. Powers
Cora Hall	Aug., 1890	C. B. Powers

Register of Communicants

Name	Comments
Mary Gains	Adm. Feb., 1867, d. in Ill.
Mariah McNeal	Adm. Feb., 1867, Dis. in Holden, Missouri
Mary M. McNeal	Adm., Feb., 1867, d. Apr. 15, 1875
Cintha A. Reeves	Adm. Feb., 1867, Dis. Shiloh, Atch. Co.
Elizabeth McAdams	Adm. Feb., 1867, d. Apr. 6, 1877, Funeral by Baird Benington
Barbara A. Williams	Adm. Feb., 1867, Moved to south Missouri
Martha Marrs	Adm. Feb., 1867, Moved to south Missouri
Salina Marrs	Adm. Feb., 1867, Moved to south Missouri
Anna E. Lackard	Adm. Feb., 1867, Gone to Ill.
Elizabeth M. NcIlroy	Adm. Feb., 1867, Trans. to Mt. Carmel, Atch. Co., MO.
Sarah E. Ferguson	Adm. Feb., 1867
Ellen Lucas White	Adm. Feb., 1867, Joined the Baptists
Parilla M. Addington (Barnhart)	Adm. Feb., 1867
Mary Morrow	Adm. Feb., 1867
Mary L. McNeal	Adm. Feb., 1867
Margaret Jones	Adm. Feb., 1867
Martha E. Starns (Trimble)	Adm. Feb., 1867, Dis. Aug. 25, 1880
Saraphine Crockett	Adm. Feb., 1867
A. J. Rhodes	Adm. Feb., 1867
Juliett T. McNeal	Adm. Feb., 1867, Dis. Rockport
Nancy J. Odell	Adm. Feb., 1867, d. Mar. 17, 1871
Sarena Good (Bowers)	Adm. Feb., 1867
Salina Plasters	Adm. Feb., 1867
M. C. McAdams	Adm. Feb., 1867

Name	Comments
Evaline Coorlane	Adm. Feb., 1867
Unice Rhodes	Adm. Feb., 1867, d. 1876
Malinda J. Garst	Adm. Feb., 1867, d. Sep. 15, 1870
Phebe A. Good (Watts)	*Adm. Feb., 1867, Moved to south Missouri

*(Note: There is a line drawn through the part about moving, with another word which might be Rutherford.)

Susannah Good	Adm. Feb., 1867
Nancy A. Smith	Adm. Feb., 1867
Sarah Smith (Barnhart)	Adm. Feb., 1867
Sarah C. Morrow (Taylor)	Adm. Feb., 1867
Clara A. Morrow (Good)	Adm. Feb., 1867
Hannah A. Addington	Adm. Feb., 1867
Josephine Matthews (Taylor)	Adm. Feb., 1867
Laura Taylor (McNeal)	Adm. Feb., 1867, Removed to Tarkio
Grace A. Cross (Warfield)	Adm. Feb., 1867
Liddie A. Sliger	Adm. Feb., 1867
Francis Bowman	Adm. Feb., 1867
Martha Bowman	Adm. Feb., 1867
Mary C. Addington	Adm. Feb., 1867
Nancy W. Eastridge	Adm. Feb., 1867
Arminta J. Reeves	Adm. Feb., 1867
Nancy Morgan	Adm. Feb., 1867 Went to Ill.
Malissa A. Reevis (Solomon)	Adm. Feb., 1867
Mary J. Cross	Adm. Feb., 1867, died in south Misouri
Arena Moor	Adm. Feb., 1867
Nancy Eastridge	Adm. Feb., 1867
Earanda Barnhart (Mann)	Adm. Feb., 1867
Angeline Jones (Lindsleg)	Adm. Feb., 1867, Went to Ill.
Anna E. Starns	Adm. Feb., 1867, Went to Tennessee
Lucy A. Morgan	Adm. Feb., 1867
Mary E. Lawson (Vanderpool)	Adm. Feb., 1867, Died in Iowa in 1876
Nancy Campbell	Adm. Feb., 1867
Mary Brown	Adm. Feb., 1867
Martha A. Barnhart (Good)	Adm. Feb., 1867
Margaret Lindsley	Adm. Feb., 1867
Ann E. Lindsley	Adm. Feb., 1867
Jane Moorland	Adm. Feb., 1867
Elizabeth Mitchel	Adm. Feb., 1867
Laura M. Helman	Adm. Feb., 1867, Went to Pennsylvania
Alice C. Helman	Adm. Feb., 1867
Emma McAdams	Adm. Feb., 1867, Joined at

Name	Comments
	Wish Grove
Nancy Trimble	Adm. Feb., 1867, Dis. Rockport
Nancy Jones	Adm. Feb., 1867, Went to Tennessee
Katherine Neuminster	Adm. Feb., 1867, Moved to Milwauka (sic)
Allie B. Duncan	Adm. Feb., 1867, Went to Ill.
Lou A. Duncan	Adm. Feb., 1867, Joined the Methodists
Sarah Hannan	Adm. Feb., 1867
Martha Miller	Adm. Feb., 1867, Moved to Rockport
Nancy T. Lee	Adm. Feb., 1867
Harrett Ross (Brozles)	Adm. Feb., 1867, Went to Iowa
Louisa Horn (Morgan)	Adm. Feb., 1867
Mary A. Rummerfield	Adm. Feb., 1867
Emma Dean	Adm. Feb., 1867
Susan Campbell	Adm. Feb., 1867
Nancy Vanderslice (Tanner)	Adm. Feb., 1867
Ambrose Addington	Adm. Feb., 1867, d. 1883
Thos. McIlroy	Adm. Feb., 1867, Sus. Oct. 29, 1877
Wm. C. McNeal	Adm. Feb., 1867 Went to Tarkio
Wm. R. Branard	Adm. Feb., 1867
Jonas Odell	Adm. Feb., 1867
John Good	Adm. Feb., 1867, d. Apr. 23, 1878
Geo. W. Walker	Adm. Feb., 1867
James McNeal	Adm. Feb., 1867, Moved to Holden, Mo.
David McNeal	Adm. Feb., 1867, Trans. to Shiloh Cong. 1884
Samuel Odell	Adm. Feb., 1867
Jefferson Eastridge	Adm. Feb., 1867, d. May 8, 1872
Ralph Morgan	Adm. Feb., 1867, d. Feb. 13, 1869
Robert Good	Adm. Feb., 1867
Henry L. Moore	Adm. Feb., 1867, Went to Texas
Mattison Barnhart	Adm. Feb., 1867, d. Aug. 15, 1872
Luther G. Ferguson	Adm. Feb., 1867
Hezekiah Barnhart	Adm. Feb., 1867
Wm. R. Morgan	Adm. Feb., 1867

Name	Comments
James Stewart	Adm. Feb., 1867
Wm. P. Brown	Adm. Feb., 1867
Daniel P. Morgan	Adm. Feb., 1867
Norton Barnhart	Adm. Feb., 1867
Abraham Helman	Adm. Feb., 1867, Went to Pennsylvania
Archibald S. Campbell	---
A. O. Nieuimister (?)	---
Harvey Duncan	Went to Illinois
John Solomon	Went to Nebraska
C. W. Harris	Went to St. Joe.
John Ross	---
Jeremiah A. York	---
Abigah Brown	Left the county
Alfred Lawson	Joined another church
Jack M. Brown	Adm. Feb., 1876, Sus. Oct. 27, 1878, Restored and trans. to Shiloh Feb., 1884.
John B. Eastridge	Adm. Feb., 1876, Sus. Jun. 20, 1877 for six months
Chas. M. Good	Adm. Feb., 1876
Robt. Bacon	Adm. Feb., 1876, Joined the Baptists
L. W. Campbell	Adm. Feb., 1876, Went to Rockport, MO
Ed. F. Reeves	Adm. Feb., 1876, Trans. to Shiloh, Feb., 1884
Abraham Bowman	Adm. Feb., 1876, Went to Kansas.
John T. Clodfelter	Adm. Feb., 1876, ranaway
Val. Johnson	Adm. Feb., 1876
Thos. Hains	Adm. Feb., 1876
Henry R. Hale	Adm. Feb., 1876, Went to Nebraska
W. L. Johnson	Adm. Feb., 1876, Left the County
Chas. R. Bushong	Adm. Feb., 1876, Sus. Dec. 22, 1878 until he repents
John H. Vanderslice	Adm. Feb., 1876
Claib J. Barnhart	Adm. Feb., 1876, trans. to Shiloh Feb., 1884
John E. Davis	Adm. Feb., 1876, trans. to Shiloh Feb., 1884
Jas. D. Vanderslice	Adm. Feb. 1876, Went to Ammajonia, Missouri
Wm. H. Morgan	Adm. Feb., 1876
Mary A. Hughs	Adm. Feb., 1876
Laura C. Barnhart	Adm. Feb., 1876

Name	Comments
Mary A. Sliga	Adm. Feb., 1876
Polly A. Barnhart (Johnson)	Adm. Feb., 1876, Dis. Oct. 15, 1877
Caroline Barnhart (King)	Adm. Feb., 1876, trans. Shiloh, Atch. Co., Mo.
Martha R. Danforth	Adm. Feb., 1876
Lou M. Martin	Adm. Feb., 1876
Sarah E. Morton	Adm. Feb., 1876
Amanda L. Morgan	Adm. Feb., 1876, Went to Lincoln, Ill., Returned Jul. 22, 1883
Loniga J. Morgan	Adm. Feb., 1876
Anna Workman	Adm. Feb., 1876, Went to Linden
Edmonia Barnhart	Adm. Feb., 1876, Dis. Oct. 15, 1877
Sarah F. Garst	Adm. Feb., 1876
Phebe M. Brown	Adm. Feb., 1876, trans. Shiloh
Martha Clodfelter	Adm. Feb., 1876, d. 1881
Sarah Hays	Adm. Feb., 1876
Elizabeth Good	Adm. Feb., 1876
Qsleize (?) E. McNeal	Adm. Feb., 1876, trans. Shiloh
Mary E. McNeal	Adm. Feb., 1876
Permelia J. Turner	Adm. Feb., 1876
Sarah A. Barnhart (Zork)	Adm. Feb., 1876
Laura M. Morgan	Adm. Feb., 1876, Went to Lincoln, IL
Mildred Rhodes	Adm. Feb., 1876, Went to Nebraska
Catharine Harris	Adm. Feb., 1876
Elizabeth Dean	Adm. Feb., 1876
Lucilla Neil	Adm. Apr. 22, 1877
Nancy Robinson	Adm. Apr. 22, 1877, Dis. Nov. 11, 1880, married Wm. Anderson
Sarah J. Young	Adm. Apr. 22, 1877
Evelen Robinson	Adm. Apr. 22, 1877
Leora A. Clark	Adm. Nov. 15, 1878, Run Off
Mary M. Goodwin	Adm. Nov. 15, 1878
Margaret Goodwin	Adm. Nov. 15, 1878
Martha J. Goodwin	Adm. Nov. 15, 1878
Mary E. Brown	Adm. Nov. 15, 1878
Hannah L. Reeves (Lawson)	Adm. Nov. 15, 1878
Sarah E. Young	Adm. Nov. 15, 1878
Mary McFarland	Adm. Nov. 15, 1878
Mary J. Reeves	Adm. Dec. 10, 1878

Name	Comments
Amis (sic) S. Smith	Adm. Dec. 10, 1878
Flora C. Winkle	Adm. Dec. 10, 1878
Nettie E. Peacock	Adm. Jan. 26, 1879, Went to Tarkio
Sarah E. Goodwin	Adm. Jan. 26, 1879
Mary M. Willon	Adm. Jan. 26, 1879
C. J. Warfield	Adm. Feb., 1879, Went to Nebraska
Hiram Hannon	Adm. Feb., 1879, Went to Nebraska
Salina C. Dunwoody	Adm. Feb., 1879
Mary E. Stifle (Clevenger)	Adm. Feb., 1879
Anna E. Hays	Adm. Feb., 1879
Casandra Hays	Adm. Feb., 1879
Minnie Good	Adm. Feb., 1879
Mary A. Stephens	Adm. Feb., 1879
Dora Eastridge (Vanderslice)	Adm. Feb., 1879
Emma Ruble	Adm. Feb., 1879
Mary Ruble (wife of A. J.)	Adm. Feb., 1879
Sarah E. Taylor (widow)	Adm. Feb., 1879
Lavina Rummerfield	Adm. Feb., 1879
Agnes Saines	Adm. Feb., 1880, Went to Ohio
Mary S. Moore	Adm. Feb., 1880
Carrie B. Warfield (Hale)	Adm. Feb., 1880, Went to Nebraska
Mary E. Campbell	Adm. Feb., 1880
Agnes E. Morgan	Adm. Feb., 1880, Went to Lincoln, Ill. Returned Jul. 22, 1883
Ada B. Peacock	Adm. Feb., 1880, Went to Tarkio
Laura J. Durham	Adm. Feb., 1880, Went to. St. Joe.
Alice E. Steritt	Adm. Jan. 1, 1881, Went to Nebraska
Adaline Browning	Adm. Jan. 1, 1881, Went to Nebraska
Dora Noble	Adm. Jan. 1, 1881
Flora B. Rhodes	Adm. Jan. 1, 1881, Went to Nebraska
Ida F. Warfield (Applegate)	Adm. Jan. 1, 1881
Anna B. Keele	Adm. Jan. 1, 1881
Mary A. Browning	Adm. Mar., 1881
Alice Thornhill	Adm. Jan., 1882
Sarah M. Addington	Adm. Jan., 1882
Dora A. Barnhart	Adm. Dec., 1882 (sic)
Minnie D. Sliger	Adm. Dec., 1882

Name	Comments
Elizabeth C. Hall	Adm. Dec., 1882
Mincie A. Hughs	Adm. Dec., 1882 trans. to Shiloh
May A. Hull	Adm. Dec., 1882, trans to Shiloh
Elizabeth J. Brown	Adm. Dec., 1882
Alice J. Shandy	Adm. Dec., 1882
Alexander McLoed	---
Jessee Sliger	---
Marion M. Good	---
John C. York	---
W. H. R. Dean	Adm. Feb., 1876
Samuel L. Manns	Sus. Jun. 2, 1877 for six months
Lafayette Morgan	---
Andrew J. Edwards	Gone to Arkansas
John Garst	---
Thos. Wm. McIlravy	---
Joseph H. Young	Adm. Apr., 1877
John Robinson	Adm. Apr., 1877
James M. Sliger	Adm. Jan. 13, 1878, trans. to Shiloh, Feb. 1884.
David Addington	Adm. Dec., 1877
John A. Broyles	Adm. May, 1878, Went to Indiana
Wm. R. C. Clark	Adm. Nov. 15, 1878, runaway
Burrel H. Goodwin	Adm. Nov. 15, 1878, trans. to Shiloh, Feb., 1884
Chas. W. Goodwin	Adm. Nov. 15, 1878, suspended
Samuel W. Dunlap	Adm. Dec. 10, 1878
Burrel Log. Goodwin	Adm. Dec. 10, 1878, d. 1883
Harvey O. Sitken	Adm. Dec. 10, 1878
John E. Smith	Adm. Dec. 10, 1878
John J. Hughs	Adm. Dec. 10, 1878
Joseph B. Goodwin	Adm. Dec. 10, 1878
Samuel O. Howlett	Adm. Jan. 26, 1879, left the county
Elisha R. Woods	Adm. Jan. 26, 1879, Went to Tarkio, Missouri
William J. Goodwin	Adm. Jan. 26, 1879
Mary E. Eastridge	Adm. Jan., 1883
Mollie Billick (Crane)	Adm. Mar., 1883
Ellenora Nox	Adm. Mar., 1883, Went to Kansas
Mary E. Hays	Adm. Dec., 1883
Laura C. Martin	Adm. Dec., 1883
May Vanderslice	Adm. Dec., 1883
Belle Vanderslice	Adm. Dec., 1883

Name	Comments
Anna Lutz	Adm. Dec., 1883
Rosa J. Prather	Adm. Dec., 1883
Mary E. Hays	Adm. Dec., 1883
Sleta A. Brown	Adm. Dec., 1883, trans. to Shiloh
Sarah D. West	Adm. Dec., 1883, trans to Shiloh
Delia A. Carter	Adm. Jan., 1884
Josephene Taylor (Vannala)	Adm. Jan., 1884
Jayne E. Hays	Adm. Jan., 1884
Sarah Raleigh	Adm. Jan., 1884
Mary C. Vanderslice	Adm. Jan., 1884
Anna Pickett	Adm. Jan., 1884
Rutha Hall	Adm. Jan., 1884
Ada M. Noels	Adm. Jan., 1884
Nellie J. Good	Adm. Feb. 8, 1885
May Morgan	Adm. Feb. 8, 1885
Rutha Good	Adm. Feb. 8, 1885

Mount Pleasant Cumberland Presbyterian Church, Virginia, Cass County, Illinois.

Church was reorganized by Benjamin Canby at the Shiloh Meeting House on December 3, 1837. The following persons were enrolled as members: Rev. Benjamin Canby, Abner Tinning, Richard Matthews, Joseph Canby, Rosanah Canby, Sarah Street, Susan Beasley, Mary Townsend Beasley, Nancy Morgan, David A. McCord, Susan B. McCord, Eliza Jane McCord, James B. Thompson, Elizabeth D. Thompson, Sarah Frasell, Sarah Lowrance, Margaret Schaeffer, William Lowrance, Richard D. Thompson, John B. Thompson, Amanda Mathews, Matilda S. Thompson, Henry Schaeffer, Catharine C. Pratt, Matilda Jane Thompson, Sarah J. Thompson.

Register of Elders

Name	Ordained	Ceased to Act
Lacklan McNiell	1844	---
Daniel Biddlecome	1868	d. 1917
Henry Bierhause	1879	---
Henry J. Campbell	1897	d. Sep. 19, 1904
John Kruse	1897	d. Mar. 5, 1946

Register of Marriages

Charles McNeil and Mary H. Paschal, (MD) May 28, 1872, (MG) Amos Cox.

Register of Infant Baptisms

Milton Bierhause, (PRTS) Thos. A. Bierhause, (BD) June 20, 1874, (MG) A. Cox.

Lorena Bierhause, (PRTS) Thos. A. Bierhause, (BD) June 20, 1874, (MG) A. Cox.

Miza (?) L. McNeill, (PRTS) C. and M. McNeill, (BD) October

11, 1874, (MG) A. Cox.
Mena M. McNeill, (PRTS) C. and M. McNeill, (BD) June 18, 1874, (MG) J. Roach.
Susanah E. Hageman, (PRTS) M. and M. Hageman, (BD) June 2, 1878, (MG) J. E. Roach.
Emma F. Cell, (PRTS) W. and N. J. Cell, (BD) June 7, 1878, (MG) J. E. Roach.
Joseph W. Cell, (PRTS) W. and N. J. Cell, (BD) June 7, 1878, (MG) J. E. Roach.
Mary E. McNeill, (PRTS) Charles and Mary McNeill, (BD) November 3, 1878, (MG) J. E. Roach.
Anna A. Hageman, (PRTS) Miller and Mary Hageman, (BD) October 30, 1881, (MG) J. E. Roach.
Sarah M. Hageman, (PRTS) Miller and Mary Hageman, (BD) October 30, 1881, (MG) J. E. Roach.
*Lola Grace, (PRTS) J. and E. Tradway, (BD) June, 1882, (MG) J. E. Roach.
   *(Note: Both the infant's and parents' names are as they appear on the offical record. On this record and the few afterwards, the child's last name is not stated.)
Norman L., (PRTS) C. and M. M. McNeill, (BD) December 16, 1883, (MG) J. A. Chase.
William H., (PRTS) M. and M. Hageman, (BD) December 16, 1883, (MG) J. A. Chase.
Raymond L., (PRTS) J. and E. Tredway (sic), (BD) November 7, 1886, (MG) John Elder.
Francis E., (PRTS) M. F. and M. Hageman, (BD) June 12, 1887, (MG) J. C. Mornyre.
Mrytle, (PRTS) John and Rosa Breck, (BD) November 24, 1889, (MG) J. C. Mornyre.
Charles L., (PRTS) Charles and M. McNeill, (BD) Mary 15, 1892, (MG) W. C. Bell.
Royal C., (PRTS) John and ROse Breck, (BD) November 12, 1893,(MG) J. N. Shelton.
Charles E., (PRTS) George and Katy Ealem, (BD) August 12, 1894, (MG) J. N. Shelton.
Ellmer Carmel, (PRTS) Edward and Anna H. Schall, (BD) October 29, 1905, (MG) J. C. Mornyre.
Eadine Nita, (PRTS) Edward and Anna H. Schall, (BD) November 28, 1897, (MG) J. C. Mornyre.
Donald J. J. Bierhouse (sic), (PRTS) J. M. and L. F. Bierhouse, (BD) February 2, 1902, (MG) D. W. Cheek.
Lizette Jane Bierhouse, (PRTS) J. M. and L. F. Bierhouse, (BD) October 23, 1904, (MG) S. Bryancor (?).
Freda Barbra (sic) Kruse, (PRTS) John and Martha Kruse, (BD) June 25, 1905, (MG) R. C. Yates.

Register of Communicants

Name	Comments
Sidney Canby	Adm. Oct., 28, 1855, d. Feb. 16, 1892
William Campbell	Adm. Sep. 1, 1856, d. Aug. 20, 1896
Margaret Carr	Adm. Mar. 2, 1862, d. May 21, 1890
Nancy Canby	Adm. Mar. 3, 1868
William Cell	Adm. Feb. 2, 1868
Mary Dorothy Campbell	Adm. Jun. 2, 1852, d. May 22, 1872
John Crother	Adm. Jan. 20, 1878, Dis. Mar. 16, 1878
Sarah F. Caywood	Adm. Feb. 15, 1880
Patric F. Caldwell (sic)	Adm. Oct. 1, 1882, d. Apr. 28, 1904
John Caldwell	Adm. Dec. 16, 1883
Emma F. Cell	Adm. Dec. 16, 1883
Lizzie Caldwell	Adm. Dec. 16, 1883, Dis. Nov. 30, 1905
Jennie Caldwell	Adm. Dec. 16, 1883, Dis. May 29, 1913
Henry J. Campbell	Adm. Sep. 18, 1887, d. Sep. 19, 1904
James Cook	Adm. Nov. 24, 1889
Pheba Clementine Cook	Adm. Nov. 24, 1889, d. Nov. 5, 1890
Katherine Caldwell	Adm. May 18, 1890, d. Nov., 1906
Ralph L. Cook	Adm. Nov. 30, 1890
Wm. L. Cook	Adm. Nov. 30, 1890
Charles E. Caldwell	Adm. Nov. 30, 1890
Wm. R. Campbell	Adm. Nov. 30, 1890, d. Aug. 10, 1895
Thomas E. Coleman	Adm. Oct. 31, 1897
Tillia Cook	Adm. Nov. 26, 1905
Frederick Cook	Adm. Nov. 25, 1913
Anna E. Davis	Adm. Feb. 3, 1870
Voluntine Davis	Adm. Feb. 7, 1875
James A. Davis	Adm. Feb. 18, 1875, Gone to Baptis (sic)
Malinda Davis	Adm. Feb. 18m 1875, Dis. Mar. 30, 1889
Edward Davis	Adm. Jan. 20, 1878
Edith A. Davis	Adm. Dec. 16, 1883, Dis. Mar. 30, 1889
August J. Derr	Adm. Nov. 30, 1890
Emma Derr	Adm. Nov. 30, 1890

Name	Comments
Minnie C. Davis	Adm. Jan. 24, 1897
Stephen Davis	Adm. Jan. 24, 1897
Estella P. Davis	Adm. Feb. 5, 1899, d. Jun. 22, 1930
Janet Davis	Adm. Feb. 5, 1899, d. Nov. 20, 1913
Charles E. Defrates	Adm. Jan. 27, 1901.
Sarah E. Davis	Adm. Nov. 25, 1913
Richard Davis	Adm. Nov. 25, 1913, d. Nov., 1957
Ethel E. Davis	Adm. Nov. 25, 1913
Lacklan (sic) McNeill	Adm. Sep. 5, 1842, d. Aug. 17, 1901
Robert McNeill	Adm. Apr. 14, 1860, d. Oct. 24, 1892
Keisah Moore	Adm. Mar. 2, 1862, d. Dec. 27, 1884
Charles McNeill	Adm. Jan. 1, 1867
William B. Millner	Adm. Feb., 1869, d. Nov. 4, 1897
Henry C. Millner	Adm. Jan. 1, 1867, Dis. Oct. 24, 1892
Amanda M. McNeill	Adm. Jan. 1, 1867
Flary McNeill	Adm. Jan. 1, 1847, d. Feb. 24, 1888
Elmira Millner	Adm. Feb., 1869
Hester Millner	Adm. Feb., 1869
Matilda J. Moore	Adm. Feb., 1870, d. Apr. 17, 1881
Alma Moore	Adm. Jan., 1871
Robert B. Moore	Adm. Feb. 4, 1877
Willard McCoy	Adm. Jan. 20, 1878
Miza J. McNeill	Adm. Dec. 16, 1883
Viena M. McNeill	Adm. Dec. 16, 1883, Dis. Jul. 12, 1901
Sariah (sic) E. Millner	Adm. Feb. 23, 1884
Robert T. Millner	Adm. Feb. 23, 1884
Edward Millner	Adm. Feb. 23, 1884
Johnah Mowery	Adm. Feb. 24, 1884
Mary Ethel McNeill	Adm. Jun. 12, 1887, Dis. Mar. 10, 1903
Lonie H. Moore	Adm. Mar. 30, 1890
Anna McGehee	Adm. May 4, 1890
Emma F. Miller	Adm. Dec. 1, 1890, Dis. Nov. 11, 1908
Edward McPhillon	Adm. Nov. 30, 1890
Mary P. Mowery	Adm. Jan. 24, 1897, Dis. Apr. 2, 1914

Name	Comments
Margaret Mowery	Adm. Jun. 13, 1897
Norman L. Merrill	Adm. Feb. 5, 1899
Amanda Atwell	Adm. Jun. 12, 1887
Caroline C. Elliott	Adm. May 18, 1890
George B. Ealam	Adm. Aug. 12, 1894
Hatty B. Ealam	Adm. Aug. 12, 1894
John F. Frame	Adm. Feb. 2, 1879
William Gans	Adm. Feb. 3, 1869
Henry Gans	Adm. Jun. 15, 1879
Darius Happers	Adm. Feb. 4, 1877
Amanda Hageman	Adm. Feb. 4, 1877, Dis. Feb. 6, 1891
Miller F. Hagemen	Adm. Mar. 17, 1878
Dora D. Henderson	Adm. Feb. 5, 1899
Thomas Johnson	Adm. Dec. 16, 1883
Mary E. Johnson	Adm. Dec. 16, 1883
Nettie A. Johnson	Adm. Dec. 16, 1883
Beacher Johnson	Adm. Feb. 23, 1884
John Kruse	Adm. Nov. 30, 1890, d. Mar. 5, 1946
Anna Kruse (Small)	Adm. Nov. 30, 1890, d. Aug. 26, 1948
Henry Kruse	Adm. Nov. 18, 1894, d. Jan. 1, 1943
Sophie Kruse (Strubbe)	Adm. Feb. 5, 1899, d. Jul. 29, 1966
David Kruse	Adm. Feb. 5, 1899, d. Feb. 6, 1962
Scytha Laman	Adm. Jun. 25, 1882
Mrs. Kate Quigg	Adm. Jun. 25, 1882
Sophia Schaeffer	Adm. Sep. 12, 1846
Eliza Schaeffer	Adm. Mar. 19, 1859
Franklin Schaeffer	Adm. Feb., 1870
Lucinda Ann Schaeffer	Adm. Feb., 1871
John W. Smith	Adm. Oct. 4, 1874
Clarinda Smith	Adm. Oct. 4, 1874
J. A. Survance	Adm. Feb. 4, 1877, d. Sep. 26, 1946
Joseph Shank	Adm. Jan. 20, 1878
Franklin Shank	Adm. Jan. 20, 1878
Rebcha (sic) Jane Sheals	Adm. Jan. 20, 1878
Mary Sheals	Adm. Oct. 1, 1882, d. Sep. 24, 1847
Mary Schmidt	Adm. Oct. 31, 1897
Rose Schmidt	Adm. Jun. 17, 1900
Title Schmidt	Adm. Jun. 17, 1900
John H. Schall	Adm. Jan. 23, 1910
Mrs. S. Schall	Adm. Jan. 23, 1910

Name	Comments
Henry Schmidt	Adm. Nov. 25, 1913
Oto Schmidt	Adm. Nov. 25, 1913
Lillie Mae Schall	Adm. Dec. 21, 1919
Hilda Schall	Adm. Dec. 21, 1919
Sarah Redpolk	Adm. Sep., 1848
Barbary Redpolk	Adm. Feb., 1869
Seranda C. Redpolk	Adm. Feb. 4, 1877
J. H. Readpath	Adm. Feb. 4, 1877
James H. Richey	Adm. Feb. 4, 1877
Ellen Reynolds	Adm. Nov. 24, 1889
Louis Roch	Adm. Nov. 24, 1913

<u>Surprise Cumberland Presbyterian Church, Clinton, Lafayette County, Missouri,</u> (Note: This church was once located in Gaines, Missouri.)

Register of Elders

Name	Ordained	Ceased to Act
Jas. Miller	Mar. 23, 1859	Jul. 7, 1872
Hugh B. Witherspoon	Mar. 23, 1859	---
Jas. E. Hutton	---	---
Joseph Simmons	Oct. 26, 1867	---
Jas. Smith	Sep. 27, 1868	d. Nov. 7, 1871
Albert Hornbeck	Sep. 27, 1868	---
John H. Parks	Jul. 27, 1870	Aug. 23, 1897
Joseph Smith	Jul. 27, 1870	---
James W. Miller	Feb. 13, 1879	---
Alex Gaines	Sep., 1896	---
Wilson Parks	Sep., 1896	---

Register of Deacons

Name	Ordained	Ceased to Act
George Nichols	Feb. 13, 1879	---
M. Read	Apr. 23, 1881	---
R. E. Trenay	---	---
Alx. Gaines	May 27, 1895	Sep., 1896
Jas. Wilson	Sep., 1896	Jun., 1899
A. L. McCoun	Sep., 1896	Jul., 1897

Register of Communicants

Name	Comments
Lucinda Gillam	Adm. Mar. 23, 1859, Dis. Mar. 7, 1871
Elizabeth Parks	Adm. 1859, Dis. Sep. 20, 1870
James Smith	Dis. Apr., 1873, d. Nov. 7, 1871 (?)
Mary Smith	Dis. Apr., 1873
Hugh B. Witherspoon	Dis. Dec. 21, 1908
Sarah A. Quick	d. 1896
James M. Miller	Adm. Aug. 24, 1859, Dis. Jul.

Name	Comments
	7, 1872, d. Apr. 5, 1896
Hetty Miller	Adm. Aug. 24, 1859, Dis. Mar., 1887
Margaret M. Miller	Adm. Apr. 27, 1859, Dis. Dec. 28, 1885
Elisa Miller	Adm. 1859, Dis. Mar. 18, 1887
Elisabeth McCown	Adm. Dec. 12, 1859, Dis. Oct. 12, 1877
Rebeca Havens	Adm. Feb. 12, 1860, d. Dec., 1897
M. Mathes	Adm. Aug. 28, 1860
Thomas C. Miller	Adm. May 25, 1867, Dis. May 28, 1876
William Gillam	Adm. Jul. 27, (?), Dis. Aug. 7, 1871
James W. Miller	Dis. Aug. 28, 1871
Jacob Gilliam	Dis. Aug. 7, 1871
F. B. Davidson	Dis. Aug. 7, 1871
Mary A. Mercer	Dis. Aug. 7, 1871
Elisa J. Dempsey	Dis. Sep. 20, 1870
Julia A. Finks	Dis. Sep. 20, 1870
Lewella M. Witherspoon	---
Susan Nichols	---
Salina Davidson	Dis. May 7, 1871
Hugh Galbraith	---
W. H. McCown	---
A. E. Witherspoon	Dis. Dec. 21, 1908
Manson B. Simmons	Adm. Jul. 27, 1867, Dis. May 27, 1870
Sarah A. Simmons	Dis. May 27, 1870
Joseph Simmons	Exp. Nov. 15, 1871
An. E. Anderson	---
Tinis P. Witherspoon	---
E. B. Dempsey	d. Feb., 1879
Anna Eliston	Dis. Nov. 15, 1871
Corneluis Williams	d. Jan., 1876
Joseph H. Smith	---
James Hutton	Adm. Jul. 29, 1867, Dis. Sep. 27, 1868
Fannie Hutton	Dis. Sep. 27, 1868
Marthy Irwin	---
Mary E. Irwin	---
Amandy E. Reed	---
Weston Dempsey	Dis. Jul. 23, 1870
Ruthy Dempsey	Dis. Apr., 1873
Albert Hornbeck	Adm. Nov. 23, 1867, Dis. Aug. 28, 1870
Mary Hornbeck	Dis. Aug. 28, 1870
Melvin McCown	Dis. Jul. 23, 1870

Name	Comments
Catherine Nichols	---
Joseph Dempsey	Adm. Feb. 28, 1869, Dis. Sep. 20, 1870
Sarah Duckworth	Adm. Feb. 28, 1869, Dis. May 17, 1879
Mary Reed	1878
John Parks	Adm. Aug. 1, 1869, Dis. Aug. 3, 1897
Zillah Parks	---
James Parks	Dis. Apr., 1875
F. A. Dory	Adm. Jan. 30, 1870
S. A. Dory	---
John E. Smith	---
Mary E. Smith	---
Susana M. Trenary	---
Nancy J. Trenary	---
Magy E. Melton	Dis. Sep., 1874
Mary A. Trenary	Adm. Jan. 31, 1870, Dis. Jun. 22, 1884
Mary C. Slavens	---
Francis E. Smith	---
Nannie J. Mills	Dis. Aug., 1875
Norwood Parks	Dis. 1876
Louisa Mills	Adm. Feb. 4, 1870, Dis. Aug., 1873
Louis Stricklan	d. Aug., 1873
Luther McCown	d. Apr., 1888
Jas. G. Fike	Adm. Mar. 27, 1870, Dis. Sep., 1873
Margret M. Fike	Adm. Mar. 27, 1870, Dis. Sep., 1873
Docena Fike	Adm. Mar. 27, 1870, Dis. Sep., 1873
George Smith	Adm. Mar. 27, 1870, Dis. Sep., 1873
Alice M. Witherspoon	Adm. Mar. 27, 1870
Alfred M. Chiles	Adm. Aug. 28, 1870, d. 1876
Amandy E. Chiles	Adm. Aug. 28, 1870, Dis. Jan. 14, 1889
Matty Chiles	Dis. Nov., 1876
Agness McKinsey	---
Cary Micklson	---
William Snider	Dis. Sep. 28, 1879
Western Trenary	Adm. Dec. 8, 1871, d. Mar., 1888
John Miller	Adm. Dec. 8, 1871, Dis. Aug., 1881
Bell Parks	Adm. Dec. 12, 1871, Dis. Feb. 12, 1881

Name	Comments
Nana J. Parks	Adm. Dec. 12, 1871, d. Aug. 22, 1874
Elisa Supeona	Adm. Dec. 12, 1871, Dis. Sep., 1874
Lelana Write	Adm. Dec. 12, 1871, Dis. 1876
Ewel H. Smith	Adm. May 7, 1871, Dis. 1887
Ethia Smith	Adm. May 7, 1871, Dis. Jan. 14, 1889
Amanda Tremary	Adm. May 7, 1871
Margaret J. Renfro	Adm. Jul. 7, 1872
Maggie Quick	Adm. Sep. 1, 1872
Mary Quick	Adm. Sep. 1, 1872
Jose Jemison	Adm. Sep. 1, 1879
George Burch	Adm. Oct. 26, 1873
Wilson Parks	Adm. Oct. 26, 1873, Dis. Aug. 3, 1897
Darius Lee	Adm. Jan. 25, 1874, d. Feb., 1878
Frederick Hammond	Adm. Jul. 25, 1874, Dis., 1897
Catharine Moore	Adm. Aug. 27, 1874
Emma Miller	Adm. Aug. 30, 1874, d. Apr., 1896
Elvina Snyder	Adm. Dec. 28, 1874, Dis. Sep. 28, 1879
Ida Smith	Adm. 1874
George Nickols	Adm. 1874
Norah S. Witherpsoon	Adm. 1874
Roseabell Johnson	Adm. Aug., 1875
Mariah ---ller	Dis. Aug., 1881
Wm. White	Adm. Jan., 1876, d. 1886
Sarah E. Bogard	Adm. Aug. 14, 1878, d. 1880
Amanda A. Trenary	Adm. Aug. 14, 1878, Dis. Sep. 8, 1878
Martin R. Snider	Adm. Aug. 14, 1878, Dis. Jun. 21, 1881
George W. Parks	Adm. Aug. 14, 1878
Rachel Bogard	Adm. Jun. 5, 1879, d. Sep., 1880
Hatty Trenary	Adm. Sep. 7, 1879
Marsh Reed	Adm. Nov., 1880
Benjamin Trenary	Adm. Aug. 27, 1881
Armilda Trenary	Adm. Aug. 27, 1881
Cynthia Riddle	Adm. Aug. 27, 1881
Laura Quick	Adm. Aug. 27, 1881
Susie Quick	Adm. Aug. 27, 1881
Catherine Hammon	Adm. Aug. 27, 1881
Elen Witherspoon	Adm. Aug. 27, 1881
William Smith	Adm. Nov. 28, 1883
P. W. Kimbrough	Adm. Jun. 22, 1884
Mrs. Sarah E. Wright	Adm. Mar. 26, 1885
Miny Hoover	Adm. Mar. 26, 1885

Name	Comments
Beney Trenary	Adm. 1890
Ben J. Gaines	---
Alexander Painis	Adm. Nov., 1892
William L. Hornback	Adm. Nov., 1892
Noah Read	Adm. Nov., 1892
Addam Ebberting	Adm. Nov., 1892
Nancy Ebberting	Adm. Nov., 1892
Sarah Trenary	Adm. Nov., 1892
John W. Fisher	Adm. Jun., 1893
Mr. C. Fisher	Adm. Jun., 1893
James W. Fisher	Adm. Jun., 1893
William Parks	Joined the Baptists
Emmuel Smith	---
Pinkney Smith	---
Albert Roberts	Adm. Nov. 4, 1896
Jas. Wilson	Adm. Nov. 4, 1896
Netty Willson	Adm. Nov. 4, 1896
Timothy Hoover	Adm. Nov. 4, 1896
Elmer J. Smith	Adm. Nov. 4, 1896
Mrs. C. Hagen	Adm. Nov. 4, 1896
P. R. Wi-----	Adm. Nov. 4, 1896
A. L. McCowen	Adm. Dec. 28, 1895, Dis. Aug. 3, 1879
Susie McCowen	---
Ida Smith	---
Albert Roberts	---

Revised Register of Communicants, Nov. 5, 1905

Name	Comments
Zillah J. Parks	Adm. Aug. 1, 1869
Elisebeth Tirrell	Adm. Mar. 10, 1860
Hattie Gaskell	Adm. Sep. 9, 1879
Sarah E. Parks	Adm. Mar. 26, 1885
George W. Parks	Adm. Aug. 14, 1878, d. Mar. 15, 1912
Bennie Trenary	Adm. 4th Sunday, Aug., 1890, d. Mar. 21, 1916
J. R. Witherspoon	Adm. Nov. 4, 1896
WIlson W. Parks	d. Mar. 11, 1912

<u>Granville Cumberland Presbyterian Church, Granville, Jackson County, Tennessee.</u>

Register of Elders

The following are listed: Hugh B. Smith (Ordained Oct. 4, 1868); J. M. Williamson; T. C. McKinley (Gone to Texas); James Hargis; Matt T. McDonald; G. R. Maddux; L. D. Ferrell; M. B. McDonnel; S. P. Burton; W. P. Grisham (Ordained about 1896).

Register of Deacons

Name	Date
Prior Grissom	May 6, 1888
William R. Watts	May 6, 1888
N. B. Myres	---
Hugh B. Hargis	June 5, 1898
J. P. Grisham	---

Register of Communicants

Name	Comments
Peggy M. Apple	---
Porter McDonald	---
James D. McKinley	---
Thiley Elder	Adm. Aug. 5, 1860
Mary J. Trousdale	---
Emily Hogan	---
Jasper J. McDonald	Adm. Aug. 3, 1860
Ridley McDonald	---
Darthuly Ferrell	---
Roda Cooper	d. Dec. 6, 1891
Thomas C. McKinley	Dis. Sep. 5, 1890
Darthuly C. McKinley	---
Mildria Burton	---
John McDonald	Adm. Aug., 1867
J. Mitchel Williamson	---
Vina Burton	---
Hugh B. Smith	Removed to Trinity
Martha A. Williamson	---
Fannie McKinley	---
Garriett D. Sadler	Adm. Oct. 3, 1869
Henry B. McDonald	---
Ann Holleman	---
Eliza Simpson	---
Matt T. McDonald	Adm. Oct. 4, 1869, Removed to Trinity
Low Ellen McDonald	Adm. Oct. 7, 1869, Joined the Methodists
* Z. Bell McDonald *(McClellan)	Adm. Oct. 7, 1869, Joined the Methodists
Susan Cooper Brown	Adm. Oct. 7, 1869
E. H. Ellen	Adm. Oct. 5, 1870, Gone to Trinity
Tennie M. McKinley	Adm. Oct. 5, 1870, Dis. Sep. 5, 1870
Van B. Dillard	Adm. Oct. 6, 1870
Elizabeth Dillard	Adm. Oct. 6, 1870
Clarissa Apple	Adm. Oct. 6, 1870
Emma J. McKinley Ferrell	Adm. Oct. 6, 1870
Margarett Holmes	---

Name	Comments
Sarah Burton	Adm. Oct. 7, 1872, Joined the Campbellites
Mary S. Reynolds	---
Latin D. Ferrell	Adm. Oct. 5, 1875
Bettie Carten (Byme)	Adm. Oct. 5, 1875
Z. Maude Holmes Page	Adm. Oct. 5, 1875
William R. Watts	Adm. Nov. 7, 1875
Valeria Sadler	Adm. Nov. 7, 1875
Emma Burton	Adm. Oct. 2, 1877, Joined the Campbellites
Mary Ferrel (Lee)	Adm. Oct. 2, 1877
Thomas L. Watts	Adm. Oct. 7, 1878
Matilda Watts	Adm. Oct. 7, 1878
*Josie Goodpasture *(Sandford)	Adm. Oct. 11, 1878
James Hargis	Adm. Oct. 13, 1878, Transfer from Sulpher Fork
Martha Draughn	Adm. Oct. 18, 1878, Dis. Jul. 28, 1890
Mary F. Grisham	---
Allice Carter	Adm. Sep. 27, 1881, Received from M. E. Church South
Winburn A. Goodpasture	Adm. Oct. 4, 1881
Jane Grisham (Pharris)	Adm. Oct. 4, 1881
John F. Burton	Adm. Oct. 14, 1883
Walter A. Holmes	Adm. Oct. 14, 1883
T. Oscar Dillard	Adm. Oct. 14, 1883
Alfred A. McDonald	Adm. Oct. 14, 1883
Laudin A. McDonald	Adm. Oct. 14, 1883
Virgil Young Salder	Adm. Oct. 14, 1883
William D. Holleman	Adm. Oct. 14, 1883
W. Frank Holleman	Adm. Oct. 14, 1883
Fannie A. Carter	Adm. Oct. 14, 1883
C. Gorda Lee (Beck)	Adm. Oct. 14, 1882, Joined the Campbellites
Wm. B. Holmes	Adm. Oct. 17, 1883
Wm. A. Hargis	Adm. Oct. 17, 1883
J. Matt, Jr.	Adm. Oct. 17, 1883
Sallie L. Smith	Adm. Oct. 17, 1883
J. Fank Bell	Adm. Dec. 2, 1883
Mary Bell	Adm. Dec. 2, 1883
Mattie J. Myers	Adm. Oct. 15, 1884
Cleora Stanton	Adm. Oct. 15, 1884
Neoma Stanton	Adm. Oct. 15, 1884
Laura Manear	Adm. Oct. 15, 1884
Tomma Mary McKinley	Adm. Oct. 15, 1884
Viola Grisham (Louis)	Adm. Oct. 15, 1884, Joined the Campbellites

Name	Comments
*Lassie Dora McKinley *(Ragland)	Adm. Oct. 15, 1884
M. Emma Morgan (Shirley)	Adm. Oct. 15, 1884
Lou Ella Bell	Adm. Oct. 15, 1884
Mahala Sadler	Adm. Oct. 16, 1884
Bell H. Lee (Watts)	Adm. Oct. 16, 1884
Cora Lee (Oliver)	Adm. Oct. 16, 1884
Floretta Grisham	Adm. Aug. 20, 1883
Ada NcDonald Holleman	Adm. Oct. 15, 1884
Leona McDonald Sadler	Adm. Aug. 16, 1884
Ella McDonald	Adm. Aug. 16, 1884, Received by experience from Trinity
Mary McDonald	Adm. Aug. 16, 1884, Received by experience from Trinity
Jo. M. Morgin	Adm. Oct. 4, 1885
Mary Apple (Ortrie)	Adm. Oct. 4, 1885
Martha A. Sellar	Adm. Oct. 6, 1885
Mrs. Bettie Manear	Adm. Oct. 7, 1885
*Bettie N. McKinley *(Beasley)	Adm. Oct. 7, 1885
*Martha J. McKinley *(Carlock)	Adm. Oct. 7, 1885, Dis. Sep. 5, 1890
Wm. M. Clark	Adm. Oct. 9, 1885
James Grisham	Adm. Oct. 10, 1885
Albert L. Holleman	Adm. Oct. 10, 1885
Aletha Tittle	Adm. Oct. 15, 1885
William D. Morgan	Adm. Oct. 15, 1885
John N. Grisham	Adm. May 5, 1886, Dis. Nov. 7, 1897
Darthina T. Grisham	Adm. May 5, 1886, Dis. Nov. 7, 1897
Miss E. T. Mabry	Adm. Oct. 5, 1886
Miss L. F. Mabry	Adm. Oct. 5, 1886
*Miss Nettie Holleman *(Dixon)	Adm. Oct. 12, 1886
Lura Smith (Vantrease)	Adm. Oct. 2, 1886
Miss Helen Dillard	Adm. Oct. 12, 1886
Miss Bebe McDonald	Adm. 1886
Miss Ila Williamson(King)	Adm. Oct. 12, 1886, d. Feb. 25, 1921
Effa Carter McDonald	Adm. Oct. 12, 1886
Edgar Dillard	Adm. Oct. 12, 1886
Miss C. A. Tittle	Adm. Oct. 12, 1886
Miss Janie Elrod	Adm. Oct. 12, 1886
Bud Simpson	Adm. Oct. 12, 1886
Mrs. Lula Holmes	Adm. Oct. 14, 1886
Mrs. M. J. Holleman	Adm. Oct. 14, 1886, Rec. from the M. E. South

Name	Comments
Miss Martha Grisham	Adm. Oct. 14, 1885, Rec. from M. E. Church South
George A. McDonald	Adm. Oct. 7, 1887
Mrs. Elizabeth Apple	Adm. Oct. 7, 1887
William C. Williamson	Adm. Mar. 4, 1888
Mrs. Martha Goolsby	Adm. Oct. 13, 1888
Maggie McKinley	Adm. Oct. 13, 1888
Jack Simpson	Adm. Oct. 13, 1888
John Hargis	Adm. Oct. 13, 1888
Maggie Holleman	Adm. Oct. 13, 1888
Sallie E. Tittle (Huff)	Adm. Oct. 13, 1888
Henry J. Stallings	Adm. May 5, 1889
Johnnie Bush	Adm. Oct. 12, 1886
J. B. Zom Tolbert	Dis. Sep. 12, 1889
N. B. Myres	Adm. Oct. 11, 1889
Nan Myres	Adm. Oct. 11, 1889
Cyntha Trousdale	Adm. Oct. 11, 1889
Lizzie Mitchel	Adm. Oct. 11, 1889
James Harris	Adm. Oct. 12, 1889
Betty D. Myres	Adm. Oct. 12, 1889
Minnie C. Williamson	Adm. Oct. 14, 1890
Altie C. Myres (Huff)	Adm. Oct. 14, 1890
John L. Dillard	Adm. Oct. 14, 1890
Robt. M. Hargis	Adm. Oct. 14, 1890
M. B. McDonald	Adm. Oct. 14, 1890
Wm. Tittle	Adm. Oct. 14, 1890
Hugh B. Smith, Jr.	Adm. Oct. 14, 1890
John Lee	Adm. Oct. 14, 1890
S. T. Burton	---
Cleo Burton	---
D. C. Simpson	Adm. Oct. 14, 1890
Wash Manier	---
Henry Myres	Adm. Oct. 15, 1890
Arvel Manier	---
Cinty Tittle	Adm. Oct. 15, 1890
Hugh Hargis	---
Adel Myers	---
Nancy Alridge	Adm. Oct. 15, 1890
Alice M. Burton (Hargis)	Adm. Oct. 10, 1893
Maggie Burton	Adm. Oct. 10, 1893
Minnie Grisham	---
Myrtle Page	---
Mrs. Lawlis	Adm. Oct. 10, 1890
William Autrie	Adm. Oct. 15, 1890
George McKinley, Jr.	Adm. Oct. 10, 1890
Homer McKinley	Adm. Oct. 10, 1890
John Simpson	Adm. Oct. 10, 1890
G. R. Maddux	---

Name	Comments
Dock Simpson	Adm. Oct. 10, 1890
Henry Myres	Adm. Oct. 10, 1890
L. Maddux	d. Jan. 27, 1897
S. P. Burton	---
A. W. Burton	---
Vetie Apple	Adm. Oct. 10, 1893
Minnie Tittle	Adm. Nov. 5, 1893
May Tittle	Adm. Nov. 5, 1893
Ida Tittle	Adm. Nov. 5, 1893
Minnie Holleman	Adm. Nov. 5, 1893

Second Revised Membership Register, (No Date)

Following members: Peggie Apple, J. D. McKinley, M. J. Trousdale, Ridley McDonald (Gone to Pleasant Hill), Ruthy McDonald (Gone to Pleasant Hill), J. M. Williamson, Thuly Elder (Quit attending church), Vie Burton, John McDonald (Gone to another church), Martha Williamson, Fannie McKinley (Dismissed by letter), Ann Holleman, Eliza Simpson (Quit going to church), Sue Brown (Dismissed by letter), Elizabeth Dillard (Dismissed by letter), Clarsie McDearman (Dead), Emma Ferrell (Dismissed by letter), Margret Holmes (Dismissed by letter), L. D. Ferrell, Bettie Byrne, Maude Page, W. R. Watts, Mary Lee (Moved out of bounds), Thomas L. Watts, Matilda Watts (d. July 1898), James Hargis, Mary Jane Carter (Adm. Jun. 16, 1903), J. P. Grisham, Prior Grisham, Martha Grisham, J. I. Apple (Gone to Pleasant Hill), Janie Pharris, John P. Burton, William Holleman (Moved out of bounds), Landon McDonald (Letter to Pleasant Hill), Alford McDonald (Gone to Pleasant Hill), Florietta Oliver (Out of bounds), W. A. Hargis, Alice M. Hargis, J. Mat Clark, Hanna Ferrell, Mary McKinley, Lassie Ragland, Mahala Sadler, Bill H. Watts, Cora Oliver, Martha Sellars, Mary Autree (Out of bounds), Bettie Beasley (Out of bounds), William Clark (Out of bounds), Eletha Tittle, W. T. Tittle, Nettie Dixon, Lura Vantrease, Helen Dillard, Effie McDonald, Mary Holleman (Out of bounds), George McDonald, Maggie McKinley, Jack Simpson (Out of bounds), John Hargis, Maggie Holleman, Sallie Huff, N. B. Myres, Johnnie Trousdale, Cynthia Trousdale, Bettie D. Myres, Minnie C. Williamson, Altie C. Huff (Out of bounds), M. B. McDonald, Maggie Burton, William Autree (Out of bounds), Homer McKinley, Hue McKinley, John Simpson, Henry Simpson, Vertie Dicken, Minnie Tittle (Huff), Mary Tittle, Idar Tittle Harris, Minnie Green, Ann Byrne, S. P. Burton, Clio C. Burton, Walter Burton, Vallie McKinley, Olda Maddux, Lizzie Maddux, Derot Burton, Hugh Hargis, Odell Myres, Minnie Grisham, Myrtle Page, Leo. Ferrell, Ed. Ferrell, Pearl Ferrell, Nallie Trousdale, Ress Eller, G. R. Maddux, Mrs. Mariah Nicholas (Out of bounds), Wm. B. Holmes (Adm. Oct. 17, 1881), Walter A. Holmes (Adm. Oct. 14, 1883), Mary Burton (Adm. Dec., 1899), Carrie Dillard (Adm. Dec., 1899), Lola

Pharris (Adm. Dec., 1899), W. W. McDonald (Adm. Jan. 7, 1900), Robt. Williamson (Adm. Jan. 7, 1900), Bettie Franklin (Adm. Jan. 7, 1900), Dora Williamson (Wife of J. F. Williamson).

Third Revised Membership Register, (No Date)

Following Members: J. M. Williamson, Vie Burton, J. P. Burton, Martha Williamson, Ann Holleman, Bettie Byrne, Thomas Watts, Bunt Byrne, Maude Page, Bill Watts, Bell Watts, James Hargis, Bettie Hargis, Prior Grisham, Martha Grisham, J. P. Grisham, Jamie Pharris (Gone to join the Methodists), W. A. Hargis, Alice M. Hargis, Hannah Hargis, Florettie Grisham, James Hargis, Jr., Martha Sellars, Lura Vantrease, Ila King, Effie McDonald, Jno. Trousdale, Minnie Hargis, Maggie Maddux, May Tittle, S. P. Burton, Clio Burton, Walter Burton, Ola Hargis, Lizzie Maddux, Dero Burton, Hugh Hargis (Joined the Methodists), Minnie Goolsby, Myrtle Page, Nallie Dennie, Ress Eller, G. R. Maddux, Lola Pharris, W. W. McDonald, Clarance Myres, N. B. Myres, Nan Myres.

Following members listed with admission dates:

Name	Admission Date
A. D. Duke	October, 1904
Nannie Duke	October, 1904
Hathie McKinnie	October, 1904
Jas. King	October, 1904
Joy Sellars	October, 1904
Mary Manley Page	October, 1904
Edith Burton	October, 1904
Lee Thompson	May, 1910
Mary Thompson	May, 1910
Eva Thompson	May, 1910
Will Thompson	May, 1910
J. C. Cowan	May, 1910
Delia Cowan	May, 1910
Onie Cowan	May, 1910
Bettie Shepherd	May, 1910
Alice Hargis	May, 1910
Effie Sadler	May, 1910
Wm. Lunday	October, 1910
Mandy Ruby Autry	August 13, 1911
Mary Nelle Ferrell	August 13, 1912
Anna Ruth Hargis	December, 1912
Etha Austin	October 12, 1913
Catharine Hargis	September 7, 1918
John L. Watts	October 5, 1919
Guy Maddux	October 5, 1919
T. D. Hargis	October 5, 1919

Fourth Revised Membership Register, (No Date)

Following Members: J. M. Williamson, W. R. Watts, James Hargis, Bell Watts, Bettie Hargis, J. P. Grisham, W. P. Grisham, Floretta Grisham, Hanna Hargis, Ola Hargis, G. R. Maddux,

Maggie Maddux, Minnie Goolsby, Lee Thompson, Will Thompson, Mary Thompson, Eve Thompson, J. C. Cowan, Delia Cowan, Annie Cowan, Bettie Shepherd, Alice Hargis, Effie Sadlar, Wm. Autree, Mary Autree, Mandy Ruby Autree, Jas. King, H. B. Knight, Mary Nell Ferrell, Anna Ruth Hargis, Etha Austin, Ila Apple, Effie Rippetoe, Margaurite Hargis, Ruby Williamson, Lilla Williamson, Henry Holleman, M. E. Gray, Susie Gray, John Watts, Guy Maddux, T. D. Hargis.

Following members listed with admission dates:

Name	Admission Dates
Minnie Hargis	d. March 13, 1921
Rebeca Dwitt Hargis	August 13, 1922
Tina Vinson	August 13, 1922
W. C. Cornwell	April, 1924
Ethel Cornwell	April, 1924
Lutrell Cornwell	April, 1924
Albert Ferrell	April, 1924
Richmond Hargis	April, 1924
Lela Maynard	April, 1924
Mattie Autry	April, 1924

Register of Adult Baptism

Name	Date	Reverend
John Trousdale	Oct. 11, 1889	C. K. Carlock
Cyntha Trousdale	Oct. 11, 1889	C. K. Carlock
Lizzie Mitchell	Oct. 11, 1889	C. K. Carlock
James Harris	Oct. 12, 1889	C. K. Carlock
Hugh Apple	Oct. 12, 1889	C. K. Carlock

Register of Marriages

W. B. Watts and Bell Lee, (MD) April 7, 1889, (MG) C. K. Carlock.

C. K. Carlock and Martha J. McKinley, (MD) August 23, 1889, (MG) G. W. Webb.

Register of Deaths

Name	Date
Sallie L. Smith	June 29, 1889
Mrs. Bill Autrey	---
Mrs. J. C. Cowan	---
Jas. Hargis	March 2, 1920
Mrs. Minni Hargis	March 13, 1922

Register of Elders

Name	Ordained Date
J. M. Williamson	d. September 22, 1929
Y. R. Maddux	1896, d. February 13, 1930
W. P. Grisham	October, 1899
Henry Holleman	First Sunday, September, 1920
W. C. Autry	May 4, 1913
Guy Maddux	First Sunday, August, 1920
John Watts	First Sunday, August, 1920
W. B. Cornwell	May 4, 1924

Name	Ordained Date	
T. D. Hargis	First Sunday, August, 1920	

Register of Pastors

Name	Installed	Resigned
Van N. Smith	August, 1917	September, 1930
--- DeHaven	October, 1930	Sept. 6, 1931
W. B. Covington	Oct. 4, 1931	---

Second Register of Deaths

Name	Death Date	Reverend
Minnie Hargis	Mar. 13, 1921	Van Smith & Dr. Smith
James Hargis	Mar. 20, 1920	Van Smith
Mrs. Will Autrey	Sep. 25, 1925	Van Smith
Mrs. Bettie Hargis	May 24, 1927	Van N. SMith
Mrs. Wynne Askew	Sep. 24, 1935	Van SMith
Mrs. J. M. Williamson	Dec. 31, 1929	Bro. N.M. Dycus
G. R. Maddux	Feb. 13, 1930	Van N. Smith
Mrs. Maude Page	Dec. 13, 1930	P. T. Evans
Mrs. Peyton Grisham	Dec. 31, 1930	Bro. DeHaven & Dr. Miller
Wynn Askew	Oct. 28, 1934	W. B. Covington
A. B. Hargis	May 26, 1935	W. B. Covington

Second Marriage Register

John L. Watts and Mary Nell Ferrell, (MD) Aug. 25, 1925, (GR RES) Akron, OH, (BR RES) Granville, TN, (W) Miss Eula Dycus and Richmond Hargis, (MG) Van N. Smith.

Walter Glenn Birdwell and Catherine Maddux Hargis, (MD) Aug. 17, 1927, (GR RES) Nashville, TN, (BR RES) Granville, TN, (MG) Van Smith.

Carl Cornwell and Ruby Williamson, (MD) ?, (GR RES) Garnville, TN, (BR RES) Granville, TN, (MG) Van Smith.

Frank Eugene Collier and Marguerite Haris, (MD) ?, (GR RES) Cookeville, TN, (BR RES) Granville, TN, (MG) Dr. Miller and Mr. DeHaven.

Register of Baptism

Marguerite Hargis, (PRTS) Mr. and Mrs. T. D. Hargis, (b.) Nov. 24, 1904, (BAPT) Age: 3Y, (Adm.) Sept. 7, 1918, (MG) Bro. S. K. Phillips.

Catharine Hargis, (PRTS) Mr. and Mrs. T. D. Hargis, (b.) Mar. 26, 1906, (BAPT) Age: 2Y, (Adm.) Sept. 7, 1918, (MG) Bro. S. K. Phillips.

Richmond Hargis, (PRTS) Mr. and Mrs. A. B. Hargis, (b.) May 5, 1908, (BAPT) Age: 7M, (Adm. Mar. 2, 1924, (MG) Bro. S. K. Phillips.

Rebecca Dewitt Hargis, (PRTS) Mr. and Mrs. T. D. Hargis, (b.) Jun. 28, 1914, (BAPT) Age: 2M, (Adm.) Aug. 30, 1924, (MG) Bro. Fount Smith.

Donald R. Maddux, (PRTS) Mr. and Mrs. Guy Maddux, (b.) Sept. 3, 1924, (Adm. Aug. 2, 1925, (MG) Bro. Van Smith.

Glen Ferrell Watts, (PRTS) Mr. and Mrs. John Watts, (b.) Jan. 28, 1928, (Adm. Oct. 7, 1928, (MG) Bro. Van Smith.

Mary Nan Huff, (PRTS) Mrs. Alta Huff, (b.) Jan. 3, 1917, (BAPT) Mar. 1, 1931, (Adm.) Mar. 1, 1931, (MG) Bro. W. B. Covington.

Register of Communicants

Name	Comments
J. M. Williamson	d. Sep. 27, 1929
Bettie Hargis	Adm. Oct. 13, 1878, d. May 24, 1927
W. P. Grisham	Adm. Oct., 1881
Floretta Grisham	Adm. Aug. 20, 1883, d. Dec. 31, 1930
Hannah Hargis	Adm. Oct. 17, 1883
Ola Hargis	Adm. First Sunday, Oct., 1893
Minnie Goolsby	Adm. Oct., 1896
G. F. Maddux	Adm. About 1894, d. Feb. 13, 1930
W. C. Autrey	Moved to Gallatin
Mary Nell Ferrell	Adm. Oct. 13, 1912
Marguerite Hargis	Adm. Sep. 7, 1918
Henry Holleman	Adm. Oct. 14, 1890
John Watts	Adm. Oct. 5, 1919
Guy Maddux	Adm. Oct. 5, 1919
T. D. Hargis	Adm. Oct. 5, 1919
Rebecca Dwitt Hargis	Adm. Third Sunday, 1924
Tina Vinson	Adm. Third Sunday, 1924, Moved Davidson County
Will Cornwell	Adm. Mar. 2, 1924
Lutrell Cornwell	Adm. Mar. 2, 1924
Albert Ferrel	Adm. Mar. 2, 1924
Lutrell Cornwell	Adm. Mar. 2, 1924
Albert Ferrell	Adm. Mar. 2, 1924
Richmond Hargis	Adm. Mar. 2, 1924
Lola Maynard	Adm. June, 1919
Mattie Autrey	Adm. Dec. 5, 1920
Cathaerine Hargis	Adm. Sep. 7, 1918, Moved to Carthage, TN
Ruby Williamson	Adm. Sep. 7, 1918
Wynne Askew	Adm. Jul. 6, 1924
Mrs. Will Autrey	Adm. Jul. 6, 1924, Moved to Gallatin
Ethel Draper	Adm. Jul. 6, 1924, Moved to Gallatin.
Ada Autrey	Adm. Aug. 7, 1924, Dis. 1927, Moved to Gallatin and joined Presbyterian Church
Franes Askew	Adm. Aug. 7, 1924

Name	Comments
Carrie Maynard	Adm. Aug. 7, 1924
Fowler Stockton	Adm. Jul. 25, 1925
Mrs. Alta Huff	Adm. Jul. 25, 1925
Mrs. Wynne Askew	Adm. Jul. 25, 1925, d. Sep. 24, 1925
Carl Cornwell	Adm. Jul. 9, 1924
Margarette Darwin	Adm. Aug. 9, 1928, Dis. to Cookeville
Rev. Van N. Smith	Adm. Sep. 22, 1927
Mrs. Van N. Smith	Adm. Sep. 22, 1927
Mrs. Claudia Blevin	Adm. Sep. 22, 1927
Mrs. A. C. Ditty	Adm. Jan. 4, 1931
Mary Frances Ditty	Adm. Jan. 4, 1931
Ila King Ditty	Adm. Jan. 4, 1931
Mary Nan Huff	Adm. Mar. 1, 1931

Original Ruling Elders Register

As Follows: Hugh B. Smith (Ordained Oct. 4, 1868), J. M. Williamson, T. C. McKinley (Gone to Texas), James Hargis, Matt T. McDonald (Membership at Trinity), G. R. Maddux (Ordained 1896), L. D. Ferrell, W. P. Grisham, M. B. McDonnel, S. P. Burton.

Revised List of Ruling Elders

As Follows: James Hargis, J. M. Williamson, G. R. Maddux, W. P. Grisham (Ordained about 1896), S. P. Burton.

Register of Deacons

Name	Ordained Date
Prior Grissom	May 6, 1888
William R. Watts	May 6, 1888
N. B. Myres	---
Hugh B. Haris	Jun. 5, 1898
J. P. Grisham	---

Crooked Creek Cumberland Presbyterian Church, Keysville, Crawford County, Missouri.

Statistical Church Record

Name	Comments
Washington Carter	d. Nov. 13, 1870, married
Catherine Carter	Married
E. H. Carter (male)	d. Sep. 17, 1871, single
Alfred Y. Carter	Single
G. W. Bullock (male)	Dis. Aug. 5, 1878
Eliza L. Bullock	Dis. Aug. 5, 1878, married
E. J. Dunlap (male)	Married, moved to SW MO
O. E. Dunlap (male)	Married, moved to SW MO
Lucinda Dunlap	Married
E. C. Dunlap (male)	Married
Polly Dunlap	Married, d. Dec. 23, 1881
Elijah Key	Married

Name	Comments
Matilda Key	Married
James N. Key	Married
Jesse B. Key	Married
Obadiah Key	Single, Sus. Jan. 9, 1876
Wm. O. Wilkerson	Married
Sarah A. Wilkerson	Married
Catharine Wilkerson	Single
George W. Browne	Age 36Y, Prof. Hopewell, Bellefountaine, Wash. Co., MO, 1847, married
Mary J. Browne	Age 31Y, Union Church, Crawford Co.
L. A. Dunlap (male)	Married, Dis. Dec. 14, 1879
Nancy Dunlap	Married, Dis. Dec. 14, 1879
A. J. Bullock (male)	Married
Wm. M. Bennett	Married, joined M.E. Church
F. J. Vaughan (male)	Married
E. J. Key (male)	Married, Restored Dec. 19, 1883
L. L. Culp (male)	Married, Dis. Nov. 14, 1879
J. E. Key	Single, Dis. Aug., 1867
Wm. E. Speer	Married, Dis. Nov., 1865
Henry Trotter	Married, d. Crawford Co.
John Dunlap	Married, d. Jan. 1, 1867, Crawford Co., MO
O. W. Carter (male)	Married, Dis. Dec. 9, 1865
Noah Angle	Married, Dis. Nov. 12, 1879
Jeremiah Key	Married
Lewis Key	Married
John Kelley	Married
H. N. Key (male)	Single, d. Aug., 1867
Wm. Baker	Married
R. A. Carter (male)	Married, Dis. Aug. 13, 1871
H. C. Vaugham (male)	Married
Jacob Humble	Married
Rebecca Bullock	Married, d. Apr. 4, 1877, Crawford Co.
Maris Dunlap	Married, d. Jan. 2, 1877, Crawford Co.
Elizabeth J. Dunlap	Married
Mary E. Key	Married, moved southwest
S. C. Dunlap (female)	Single, d. Aug. 26, 1878
Harriett E. Dunlap	Single, d. Mar. 16, 1877, Crawford Co.
Mirah D. Vaughan	Married
Margaret H. Dunlap	Single, Dis. Oct., 1865
Matilda A. Key	Married
Mary H. Carter	Married, Dis. Feb., 1866

Name	Comments
Sarah J. Baker	Married
Charlotte Burton	Single, Dis. Dec., 1865
Nancy Kelly	Married
Ann A. Wilkerson	Single, Dis. Jan. 23, 1880
Martha E. Carter	Single
Martha E. Harman	Married, Dis. Jan. 20, 1872
Susan Culp	Married
Susan Eaton	Married
Lewis Key	Restored Sep. 20, 1874
William Key	Married
Elvira Key	Married
Sarah E. Russell	Married, Dis. Mar. 12, 1881
Isaac E. Key	Single, Bapt. by A. O. Melvin
Welshy Ann Keller	---
Jennie Key	Single, Bapt. by E. M. Johnson
Rosa Key	Married
Obadiah Key	Single
Samuel A. Key (male)	---
Lutie Dunlap	Single, Never Bapt.
L. P. Key (male)	Married, Bapt. Dec. 19, 1883, by Rev. J. Campbell
Louisa J. Key	Married, Bapt. Dec. 19, 1883, by Rev. J. Campbell
Mary E. Key	Single, Bapt. Dec. 19, 1883, by Rev. J. Campbell
Nora Key	Single, Bapt. Dec. 19, 1883, by Rev. J. Campbell
Laura Key	Single, Bapt. Dec. 19, 1883, by Rev. J. Campbell
Mantra Butt	Single, Bapt. Dec. 19, 1883, by Rev. J. Campbell
Lulie Butt	Single, Bapt. Dec. 19, 1883, by Rev. J. Campbell
Jas. Davis	Married, from Canaan, Prf. Faith at Cook Station, Bapt. Dec. 19, 1883.
Matilda Davis	Married, from Canaan, Prf. Faith at Cook Station, Bapt. Dec. 19, 1883
Mark L. Butt	Married, formerly Methodist, Bapt. Dec. 19, 1883
Matilda A. Butt	Married, Bapt. Dec. 19, 1883
Samuel Duncan	Single, Bapt. Dec. 19, 1883
John Powell	Married, Bapt. Dec. 19, 1883, by Rev. J. Campbell
Malissa R. Key	Single, Bapt. Dec. 19, 1883

Shady Grove Cumberland Presbyterian Church, Wingo, Graves County, Kentucky.

Register of Names

Name	Comments
Mary A. Mary	---
R. L. Jones	---
M. R. Jones	---
J. E. Holmes	Adm. September 10, 1882
J. B. Wagoner	---
Lillie Oliver	Adm. August 18, 1882
Mary Wagoner	---
Rose Walker	Adm. September 19, 1884
Mollie Alexander	---
N. J. Holmes	---
J. D. Alxander	Adm. August 14, 1881
Addie Batts	Adm. September 13, 1885
Lucy Jones	Adm. September 13, 1885
Della Chaney	Adm. September 13, 1885
Cora Garrett	Adm. September 13, 1885
Roxie Martin	Adm. October 19, 1886
M. F. Jones	Adm. October 19, 1886
R. R. Coplin	Adm. August 21, 1887
James Anderson	Adm. August 21, 1887
Lula Pritchard	Adm. August 22, 1887
W. D. Coplin	Adm. August 22, 1887
J. P. Holmes	Adm. August 17, 1889
Isaac Adams	Adm. August 17, 1889
B--li- Coplin	Adm. October 15, 1892
J--- Byron	Adm. April 19, 1893
--- Coplin	Adm. April 19, 1893
--- Coplin	Adm. April 19, 1893
--- Byron	Adm. August 19, 1893
--- Mullens	Adm. August 19, 1893
---in Mullens	Adm. August 19, 1893
Lula Holefield	Adm. August 19, 1893
Annie Redden	Adm. August 19, 1893
Lottie Holmes	Adm. August 19, 1893
Cornelius Holmes	Adm. August 19, 1893
Walter Wagoner	Adm. August 20, 1893
Bell Brown	Adm. August 20, 1893
Wayland Adams	Adm. August 20, 1893
Byrd Alexander	Adm. August 22, 1893
Tilman Jones	Adm. August 25, 1893
--- Wagoner	Adm. August 21, 1894
Lura Mullens	Adm. August 21, 1894
J. R. Smith	Adm. August 21, 1894
Laura Holmes	Adm. August 21, 1894
Naomie Bradley	Adm. August 21, 1894
Manda Bradley	Adm. August 21, 1894

Name	Comments
Martha Coplin	Adm. October 14, 1889
Livina M. Wagoner	Adm. August 17, 1889
J. A. Jones	Adm. August 17, 1889
Albert Richie	Adm. August 20, 1899
Nellie Holmes	Adm. April 10, 1900
R. N. P. Fields	Adm. August 13, 1900
Nellie Bradley	Adm. August 28, 1901
Rose Watson	Adm. August 28, 1901
Lury B. Tucker	Adm. August 28, 1901
Mabel Oliver	Adm. August 28, 1901
Cordie Jones	Adm. August 28, 1901
Letha Holmes	Adm. August 28, 1901
E. R. Bradley	Adm. August 28, 1901
Dona Bradley	Adm. August 28, 1901
Tom Holifield	Adm. August 28, 1901
Bertha Walker	Adm. August 28, 1901
Charlie Holmes	Adm. August 28, 1901
Otto Alexander	Adm. September 15, 1901
F. C. Mays	Adm. September 15, 1901
Eva C. Nichols (Jones)	Adm. September 15, 1901
Mrs. Mary Tucker	Adm. July 25, 1902
Pearl Martin	Adm. August 17, 1902
Lena Mays	Adm. September 16, 1902
Charlie Choate	Adm. September 17, 1903
Della Jones	Adm. September 17, 1903
R. A. Sutton	Adm. September 17, 1903
Frank Jones	Adm. September 17, 1903
Willard Byrn	Adm. September 17, 1903
J. B. Jones	Adm. October 19, 1903
Mary Holmes	Adm. August, 1904
Mrs. Nannie Byrn	Adm. August 9, ????
Mary F. Waggoner	Adm. August 15, 1909
J. H. Waggoner	---
---by Choate	---

Delinquent List

Name	Comments
L. B. V. Thomson	---
Addie Melton	August 28, 1893
Callie Keland	August 20, 1893
Kate Thomson	August 20, 1894
Andrew Martin	August 20, 1894
Neal Caham	August 20, 1894
Mrs. Calhoun	August 20, 1894
Newt Pitison	August 20, 1894
Minnie B. Coplin	August 28, 1901
Fannie Taylor	August 28, 1901
Etta Kelan	August 28, 1901
William T. Wagoner	August 28, 1901

Name	Comments
Mrs. N. J. Wgoner	August 28, 1901
Hilry Taylor	August 28, 1901

Post Oak or Spence's Chapel, Sugar Tree, Decatur County, Tennessee.

Register of Elders

Name	Ordained	Ceased to Act
J. K. P. Agnew	Aug. 11, 1886	Feb. 14, 1897
S. C. Roberson	---	Feb. 14, 1897
John Lamrock	---	d. Aug. 16, 1903
J. W. McSullivan	Oct. 26, 1890	Jun., 1900
G. M. Thorton	Mar. 18, 1876	Jun., 1900
James Wilson	Sep. 7, 1894	---
Wm. Gronamiah	Nov. 22, 1896	Aug. 29, 1899

Register of Deacons

Name	Ordained	Ceased to Act
T. C. Roberson	Apr. 15, 1876	May 23, 1896
J. F. Farlon	Aug. 27, 1896	Feb. 14, 1897
J. H. Harris	Aug. 27, 1896	---
Miss Mary Thomas	May 28, 1899	---

Register of Communicants

Name	Admission Date
Adia Egnew	August 11, 1886
F. A. Cox	May 5, 1886
F. E. Prince	May 5, 1886
Enola Barr	August 6, 1886
F. F. McIllwain	October 9, 1887
M. A. McIllwain	October 9, 1887
M. E. F. Roberson	October 9, 1887
L. L. Roberson	October 9, 1887
L. D. Roberson	October 9, 1887
W. M. Gronamiah	April 8, 1886
Nancie Wheat	August 9, 1889
Joseph Wheat	August 9, 1889
Mary Jane Tharnton	August 11, 1889
E. L. Odle	August 11, 1889
John Barr	August 11, 1889
I. McIllwain	August 11, 1889
S. G. McIllwain	August 11, 1889
R. J. Roberson	September 7, 1891
L. L. Cox	September 6, 1891
J. L. Newsom	September 6, 1891
Mary Thomas	September 6, 1891
Veta Thorton	October 1, 1893
Jennie Roberson	October 1, 1893
James Willson	September 1, 1894
Samuel Willson	September 1, 1894
Walter Cox	September 1, 1894

Name	Admission Date
Crawford Briggance	September 1, 1894
Lillie Briggance	September 1, 1894
Martin Hancock	September 1, 1894
Layfaytte Tippett	September 1, 1894
Beaulah B. Akin	September 1, 1894
Emmeline Collette	September 1, 1894
M. C. Collette	September 1, 1894
Louisa Box	September 1, 1894
J. W. Briggance	September 2, 1894
J. F. Farlow	September 16, 1894
S. J. Wesson	September 16, 1894
Jennie Wesson	September 16, 1894
R. D. Bawcum	October 3, 1894
Mollie Farlow	October 28, 1894
Nannie Wesson	October 28, 1894
M. D. Odle	October 28, 1894
W. T. Robison	October 28, 1894
Joseph Odle	October 28, 1894
Frances L. Morris	July 30, 1895
Eliza M. May	July 30, 1895
Jessie G. Callett	July 30, 1895
Joseph H. Harris	July 30, 1895
Florance Harris	July 30, 1895
E. T. Deason	July 30, 1895
Sarah Deason	July 30, 1895
Idar A. Morris	September 6, 1895
Lavenia A. Morris	September 6, 1895
W. T. Mosely	March 2, 1896
James O. Oatswall	August 27, 1896
Aredell H. Oatswall	August 27, 1896
C. E. Bohanan	September 16, 1897
M. L. Bohanan	September 16, 1897
H. E. Newsom	September 16, 1897
Pearlie Sanders	September 16, 1897
Victoria Newsom	September 16, 1897
Sarah Thomas	September 16, 1897
G. M. Newsom	September 17, 1897
C. C. Newsom	September 17, 1897
Lovis Sanders	September 17, 1897

The following persons were on the register, but did not have an admission date: Jane Wilson, Malinda Akin, Mary Wesson, E. J. Thornton, Suson (sic) McIllwain, Mary Akin, Sarah Cox, Racheal Newsom, Eliza Odle, Eliza J. F. Roberson, Sarah Lamrock, Mary L. McIllwain, Elizabeth Thornton, J. D. Cox, Jane Cox, Martha Cox, E. J. Gronamiah, S. J. Cox, M. A. Thornton, Elizabeth Cox, A. M. Thornton, Viola Odle, John Cox, S. J. Wesson, Saraheta Spence, Roda Roberson, Mary Jane Kirk, S. D. Newsom, Irodell Thornton, Sarah Roberson, C. T. Wheat, J.

F. Kirk, W. G. Fry, Jennie Fry, J. L. Cox, Sallie Newsom, Sarah Massey.

Register of Deaths

Name	Death Date
Rachel Newsom	July 12, 1896
E. T. Deason	July 5, 1897
John Cox, Sr.	April 27, 1898
John Lamrock	August 16, 1903
Sarah Lamrock	---
A. M. C. Gassett	April 8, 1907
Pearlie Frazier	July 27, 1911
Louise Gassett	May 1, 1913
D. A. Gassett	September 23, 1922

Register of Marriages

(Note: On these first three marriage records the groom's name was the same.)

J. W. Briggance and Eliza B. Cox, (MD) August 20, 1892, (MG) H. Franks.

J. W. Briggance and Kate Thornton, (MD) Apr., 1894, (MG) ?.

J. W. Briggance and Veda Thornton, (MD) Dec., 1894, (MG) ?.

Lena Cox, (MD) Feb., 1894. No Groom listed.

W. S. Petty and L. L. Robison, (MD) May, 1896, (MG) A. P. Spence.

T. F. Fisher and M. A. McIllwain, (MD) September 10, 1899, (MG) R. W. Gassett.

G. R. Newsom and H. E. Miller, (MD) Jan., 1897.

Fird Malin and Katie McIllwain, (MD) ?, (MG) --- Franks.

Register of Adult Baptisms

Name	Date	Reverend
J. I. McEllwain	Oct., 1890	A. M. O. Gossett
S. G. McIllwain	Oct., 1890	A. M. O. Gossett
Vela Thornton	Oct. 1, 1893	E. R. Deason
James Willson	Sep. 1, 1894	E. R. Deason
Walter Cox	Sep. 1, 1894	E. R. Deason
Crawford Briggance	Sep. 1, 1894	E. R. Deason
Martin Hancock	Sep. 1, 1894	E. R. Deason
Lafayette Tippett	Sep. 1, 1894	E. R. Deason
Beaulah Akin	Sep. 1, 1894	E. R. Deason
Emmeline Collette	Sep. 1, 1894	E. R. Deason
M. C. Collett (sic)	Sep. 1, 1894	E. R. Deason
Louisa Box	Sep. 1, 1894	E. R. Deason
Lillie Briggance	Oct. 7, 1894	A. M. O. Gossett
J. F. Farlow	Sep. 16, 1894	E. R. Deason
S. J. Wesson	Sep. 16, 1894	E. R. Deason
Jennie Wesson	Sep. 16, 1894	E. R. Deason
R. D. B----on	Oct. 28, 1894	E. R. Deason
Frances Morris	Jul. 30, 1895	E. R. Deason
Je--- Y. Collett	Jul. 30, 1895	E. R. Deason
Idar A. Morris	Sep. 6, 1895	A. M. O. Gossett

Name	Date	Reverend
J. O. Oatswall	Aug. 27, 1896	W. T. Mosely
H. H. Oatswall	Aug. 27, 1896	W. T. Mosely
Pearlie Sanders	Sep. 17, 1897	W. T. Mosely
Levi Sanders	Sep. 17, 1897	W. T. Mosely
Ellen Ruddie	Sep. 17, 1897	W. T. Mosely
Sarah Thomas	Sep. 17, 1897	W. T. Mosely
Victoria Newsom	Sep. 17, 1897	W. T. Mosely
C. C. Newsom	Sep. 17, 1897	W. T. Mosely
Mary E. Waters	Sep. 2, 1903	J. G. Anderson
Osco Cox	Sep. 4, 1903	J. G. Anderson
Minnie Hamilton	Sep. 4, 1903	J. G. Anderson
Alma Harris	Sep. 5, 1904	J. G. Anderson
Oma Bawcum	Sep. 5, 1904	J. G. Anderson

Rochester Cumberland Presbyterian Church, Helena, Andrew County, Missouri.

Register of Elders

Name	Ceased to Act	Ordained
Henry Blanket	---	Jun. 11, 1871
Wm. Hayter	1875	---
S. A. Irvin	---	---
George Loues	1875	Jun. 17, 1871
M. V. Piper	1874	Jun. 17, 1871
W. P. Slade	---	---
John J. Signist	---	1875
M. R. Mickles	---	Feb., 1892
J. F. Martin	---	Jun., 1892
Henry Maddock	---	Jun. 24, 1896
George Tethro	---	Jun. 24, 1896
Jas. D. Elder	---	Jun. 24, 1896

Register of Deacons

Name	Ordained	Ceased to Act
W. M. Shanks	Jun. 17, 1876	d. 1878
D. G. Caldwell	Feb., 1892	d. 1898
Lura Wiloughby	Mar., 1894	d. 1907
Mrs. M. F. Nuckols	Mar., 1894	d. Jan. 8, 1932

Register of Marriages

L. Buler and Sophia Slade, (MD) October 2, 1870, (MG) A. Guthery.

James S. Blount and Flora Simmons, (MD) October, 1874, (MG) C. B. Powers.

Register of Deaths

Name	Death Date
Sarah McLathlue	April 19, 1878

Register of Adult Baptism

Name	Date	Reverend
Mrs. C. Frame	Mar. 20, 1871	Layette Munkers
Edward B. Willoby	Mar. 20, 1871	Layette Munkers

Name	Date	Reverend
Susan A. Shanks	Mar. 20, 1871	Layette Munker
Susannah Shreve	Mar. 20, 1871	Layette Munker
Elizabeth E. Peper	Mar. 20, 1871	Layette Munker
Price Summers	Mar. 20, 1871	Layette Munker
Wm. Hector	Mar. 20, 1871	Layette Munker
Laura Mitchel	Mar. 20, 1871	Layette Munker
William Piper	Mar. 20, 1871	Layette Munker
Mary Slade	Mar. 20, 1871	Layette Munker
Rhoda Piper	Mar. 20, 1871	Layette Munker
Mrs. Sallie Brown	Mar. 20, 1871	Layette Munker
Charles McGlothlin	Mar. 20, 1871	Layette Munker
Martin V. Piper	Jun., 1871	Layette Munker
Louisa Piper	Jun., 1871	Layette Munker
Louisa Hayter	Feb., 1870	A. W. Guthery
Psafine (?) Fales (?)	Mar. 20, 1871	Layette Munker
James Blount	Nov., 1872	Layette Munker
Alice Metcalf	Nov., 1872	Layette Munker
Mrs. Belton	Jul., 1872	Layette Munker
Susan Osburn	May, 1872	Layette Munker
Wm. Cook	Jan., 1874	T. M. Miller
Hannah E. Cook	Jan., 1874	T. M. Miller
Maud Jayne	Jan. 29, 1893	J. S. Wayman
Claud Caldwell	Jan. 30, 1893	J. S. Wayman
Earl Bloomer	Oct. 29, 1899	H. W. Fisher
Thos. N. Jaynes	Oct. 29, 1899	H. W. Fisher
Ruby Bloomer	Oct. 29, 1899	H. W. Fisher

Register of Communicants

Name	Comments
H. H. Blount	Adm. Sep. 5, 1870
Mrs. H. Blount	Adm. Aug. 7, 1870
James S. Blount	Adm. Sep., 1871
Geoganna Baker	Adm. Jan. 24, 1872, Dis. 1874
Mrs. Sarah Brown	Adm. Jan. 17, 1871
Mary Baker	Adm. Mar. 22, 1871, Dis. 1874
Miss Psaphene File	Adm. Aug. 7, 1870, Dis. 1872
Wm. Frame	Adm. Mar. 20, 1871, d. 1884
Elizabeth Belton	Adm. Apr., 1872
Mrs. Joannah Grey	Adm. Sep. 18, 1870, d. 1871
Mrs. Sarah Page	Adm. Mar. 20, (?)
Mrs. Elvira P. Hicklen	Dis. 1882
Wm. Hayter	Adm. Aug., 1867, Dis. 1879
Louisa Hayter	Adm. May, 1868
James H. Hill	Adm. Nov., 1867, d. 1874
Margaret Hill	Adm. Nov., 1867, d. 1874
Wm. Hector	Adm. Mar. 20, 1870
Jane Hector	1872
Henry Boltzer	Adm. Jan. 23, 1874, d. 1874
S. A. Irwin	---

Name	Comments
Isabel J. E. Irwin	Adm. Aug., 1868
Joseph Irwin	Adm. Aug., 1868
R. A. Irwin	Adm. Apr. 21, 1872
Sarah I. Irwin	Adm. Aug., 1868
Wm. Cook	Adm. Mar., 1871, d. 1873
Hannah Cook	Adm. Mar., 1871, d. 1873
Malinda Cook	Adm. Mar., 1871, d. 1873
George W. Louis	Adm. Aug. 7, 1870, Dis. 1878
Susannah Louis	Adm. Aug. 7, 1870
Lena Louis	Adm. Aug. 7, 1870, Dis. 1878
Elizabeth Millaken	Adm. May, 1868
Elizabeth McGlothlen	Adm. Mar., 1871, d. 1870
Charles McGlothlen	Adm. Mar., 1871, d. 1879
Sarah McGlothlen	Adm. Feb., 1871, d. Apr., 1878
Laura Mitchell	Adm. Mar., 1871, Dis. Jan. 20, 1873
Alice Medcalf	Adm. Sep., 1871, Dis. 1872
Henry Mattox	Adm. Jan. 24, 1872
Mrs. Jenny Mattox	Adm. Jan. 24, 1872
Francis Patton	Adm. Feb., 1868
Clarissa Patton	Adm. Aug., 1868, Dis. 1879
Margaret Patton	Adm. Aug., 1868
Marten U. Piper	Adm. Mar., 1871, Dis. 1878
Elizabeth C. Piper	Adm. Mar., 1871, Dis. 1878
Wm. Piper	Adm. Mar., 1871, Dis. 1882
Rhoda Piper	Adm. Mar., 1871, Dis. 1882
Cyntha Ann Piper	Adm. Mar., 1871, Dis. 1882
Mrs. Louisa Piper	Adm. Jun. 17, 1871, Dis. 1882
Eliza Patton	Adm. Apr. 21, 1872, Dis. 1876
W. W. P. Slade	Adm. Sep., 1854
Isabel Slade	Adm. Aug., 1840
Elizabeth Slade	Adm. Mar., 1871
Achcy (?) Shrete	Dis. 1881
Lucy Simmons	Adm. Aug., 1868, Dis. 1878
Sophiah SLade	Adm. Aug., 1868
F. A. Simmons	Adm. Aug. 7, 1870, Dis. 1878
Lucinda Simmons	Adm. Mar. 20, 1871
Anna Catharine Sharp	Adm. Aug. 7, 1870, Dis. 1873
Mrs. Mary Signist	Adm. Aug. 7, 1870
J. S. Sharp	Adm. Sep. 6, 1870, Dis. 1873
Frances E. Shrieves	Adm. Sep. 6, 1870
Catharine Signist	Adm. Sep. 6, 1870
Mary A. Shrieves	Adm. Sep. 6, 1870
Emma Sharp	Adm. Sep. 6, 1870, Dis. 1873
Rachel Scott	Adm. Sep. 6, 1870, Dis. 1874
Mary Slade	Adm. Mar., 1871
M. M. Shanks	Adm. Feb., 1871
Susan A. Shanks	Adm. Feb., 1871

Name	Comments
Price Summers	Adm. Feb. 20, 1871, Dis. 1871
Rebecca Sale	Adm. Feb. 20, 1871
Marshel Shint (?)	Adm. Feb., 1871
John P. Sigrist	Adm. Mar. 20, 1871, Dis. 1873
Armina Shrite	Adm. Sep., 1872
Lucinda Shreve	Adm. Apr., 1872
Jonathan Snowden	Adm. 1874
Henry B. Turner	Adm. Sep. 6, 1870, Dis. 1873
Amanthe J. Turner	Adm. Sep. 6, 1870, Dis. 1873
Sarah Tumbleson	Adm. Sep. 6, 1870, Dis. 1873
Mrs. Tethro	Adm. Sep. 6, 1870
Edward B. Willoughby	Adm. Mar. 20, 1871, Dis. 1879, d. 1881
Armenta Woodard	Adm. Aug. 7, 1870
Ferneler (?) Woodward	Adm. Sep. 6, 1870
J. R. Williams	Adm. Mar., 1872

Beaver Creek Cumberland Presbyterian Church, Beaver Creek, Knox County, Tennessee, (This book was in very poor condition).

Register of Elders

As Follows: Thomas Wilson, Alexander Gaston, Maxell Brown, Henry J. Yarnell, James H. Norman, Andrew Thompson, James J. Bell, Alexander M. Hall, Thomas Collier.

Register of Lay Members

Name	Comments
Eleanor Gaston	d. October 26, 1841
James Dowlin	d. July 12, 1859
Hannah Wood	d. March 29, 1858
Sarah York	d. August 19, 1835
Kathaerine Julien	Married now K. Yarnell
Tabitha	Woman of color, d. 1855
Ann Dowlin	Married now Ann Dobens
Susan York	Married now Susan Far
Nancy	Girl of Color
James J. Bell	d. Sep. 4, 1841
Nancy Allred	Married now Nancy Branan
Tabitha Staley	Married now Tabitha Norman
Margaret E. Brown	Married now Margaret E. Groner
John Wilson	d. 1846
Hannah Stailey	Married now Hannah Cooper
Elizabeth Dann	Married now Elizabeth Williams
--- Dowlen	Married now Jane Brown
--- Ann Dowlen	Married now M. A. Roberts
--- E. Bell	Married now Nancy E. Lones
--- J. Bell	Married now M. H. J. Johnson
--- Brown	Married now J. Collier, d. Jul. 25, 1861

Name	Comments
James H. Roolen	Suspended May 10, 1845
Blackston L. Bell	d. Mar. 22, 18??
Mary Ann Bell	Married now Mary Ann Murry
Winny Williams	d. Feb. 11, ????
Elijah Jennings	d. Mar. ??, 1865
Sarah	Girl of color belonging to S. B. West
Kesia	Girl of color belonging to Mary Wilson
Rachel Jenings	d. Mar. 12, 1865
Rebecca Jane Nicholson	Married now R. J. Brown, d. Aug. 12, 1861
Sarah Ann Cox	Married now S. A. Coward
Elizabeth Brown	Married now E. Tilery
--- J. Ring	Married now M. J. Mangum
--- Dowlen	Married now L. A. Garner
--- Bell	Married now E. J. Mcrennolds
---gham (?)	d. 1862
Mary E. Dowlin	Married now M. E. Wilkins
Catharine J. Groner	Married now C. J. Edington
Henry C. A. Crowford	Joined the Methodists
Mary E. Bell	Joined the Baptist
John W. Carter	d. Aug. 10, 1872
Amanda West	Girl of color, joined the Methodist
Eliza Bell	Girl of color, joined the Methodist
Sarah Fox	Girl of color, joined the Methodist
Abselem Norman	Joined the Baptist
Thomas	Man of color
Mrs. Chineworth's Jim	Man of color
Joseph Black's Hand	Man of color

The following lay members were listed without comments of genealogical value: Nancy Norman, Mary Ann Scarbrough, Ailcy Norman, John York, Susan McLain, Elizabeth Dowlin, Thomas Bell, Eleanor Bell, Mary Taylor, Emily Bradley, Adam Smith, Barbara York, Mary Keasling, Frances Keasling, Elijah Bradley, Margaret Harper, Margaret C. Bell, Katharine Norman, Elizabeth Norman, Daniel Wood, Sarah Wood, Isaac T. Naff, Tho. Collier, Christenberry York, Joseph W. Allred, Sarah R. York, Katharine Stout, Mary York, Achsah (?) Robertson, Joseph A. G. Brown, Rebecca Collier, Alexander M. Hall, Martha Hall, Mary Lones, Deborah Nicholson, --- Kernell, --- Moore, --- Stailey, John Cox, Alexander Brown, Jane Brown, Sarah Julien, Ebenezer Julien, Samuel P. Bell, Richard S. Bell, Samuel M. Love, James Collier, James B. Brown, Martha Dowlen, John M. Davis, Jane S. Davis, Joseph A. Pyatt, Hardy F. Marshall, John Malone, Jane

Riley, ELizabeth A. Bell, Sarah Norman, Julia Ann York, Susan Bell, John M. Brown, John West, Jane Kernell, Sarah Jenings, James Cooper, Elizabeth Williams, Hardy M. Brown, Deborah Nicholson, Mary Shockey, Barby Ann Norman, Francis M. Bell, Washington Bell, -- M. Bell, -- J. Bell, --- Arnold, James S. Dowling, -- W. Brown, -- J. Ring, Samuel M. Bell, Nancy E. Murray, Josiah Murray, Robert Murray, John Murray, James Cox, M. B. Collier, Nancy Boildon, Nancy Wilkenson, Lucinda Marshall, David Biram, Sopiah Potter, Elizabeth J. Cox, Margaret Shelton, Joseph Garner, Tabitha Cooper, John Garner, Mary Isabel Groner, James Black, Elizabeth Black, Emaline Brown, David Coward, George Wilkinson, John Wilkinson, Joseph Cox, Elizabeth Cox, John Duncan, John Black, F. M. Bell, Mary Emaline Bell, M. L. Berry, Rebecca Berry, John M. Roberts, Samuel M. C. Cooper, Allen Dalrymple, Henrietta Dalrymple, Calvin Robbins, LOuana Robbins, R. --- Parker, David Johnson, Alexander Chenoweth, Thomas Brown, Nancy Herington, Charles Nelson, M. A. Parker, Fanny Murray, Baxter Groner, Russell Groner, Russell Groner, H. M. Brown, Elizabeth Brown, Ellen Brown, Merinda Bell, Mary E. Bell, James A. Bell, Mary Shelton, Jackson Lea, Isiah Usiah Norman, Sarah Marshall, V. M. Presnell, Mary Staten, J. D. Reynolds, --- H. Bell, Horace E. Irish, L. F. Brown, J. G. Armstrong, William McElroy, Lilly A. McElroy, Joel Jennings, Tempy Presnell, Ell Israel, Sofrona E. Mays, Mary Mays, Isaac Presnell, Joseph Edington, Susan Norman, Sarah Houser, Martha Reed, M. A. Wilkerson, Catharine Brown, W. W. Wilkerson, Ellen Ellis, Luly Lucy, Thomas Cooper, Isabel Cooper, Lizzy Knox, Tennesse Edington, George A. Collier.

<u>Rock Springs or Oak Grove Cumberland Presbyterian Church, Hector, Pope County, Arkansas.</u>

Register of Elders

Name	Ordained
F. M. Lenlez	April, 1879
J. M. Hollybaugh	May, 1880
Ephraim Hill	May, 1880
W. F. Rose	February, 1882
Wiley Burns	August 20, 1882
J. M. Henkle	August, 1875
L. M. Coretall	August 20, 1882
T. M. Poe	May 10, 1887, resigned July 29, 1899
D. N. Craig	---
P. W. Grinder	---
T. J. Shreve	September 11, 1892
Charley Price	d. 1895
A. L. Baley	---
R. L. Hamilton	Sus. November 5, 1894

Name	Ordained
W. H. Burns	d. 1897
Chas. Price	October 2, 1892, d. July 29, 1899
C. C. Turnsboro	d. February 25, 1895
J. H. Hurley	August, 1899
A. S. Kinsloy	August 2, 1899, Ceased to act September, 1901
G. W. Bushing	---
G. W. Eubanks	---

Register of Deacons

Name	Ordained
Hanry Bailey	September 11, 1892
R. M. Poe	September 11, 1892
H. W. Rowland	September 11, 1892, Ceased to act, 1892.
J. D. Shreve	d. January 11, 1892
J. H. Hurley	February 5, 1893, Ceased to act August 2, 1899
W. J. Johnson	---
C. H. Reavis	November 27, 1884
S. R. Hurley	---
G. W. Eubanks	November 27, 1884

Register of Marriages

Alex Story and Polly Hawkins, (MD) June 27, 1882, (MG) W. W. Watkins.

R. M. Poe and Ella Tacket, (MD) September 4, 1892, (MG) Joe A. Smith.

Chas. Price and Viola Taclet, (MD) February 24, 1893, (MG) W. W. Watkins.

Lee Bullock and Noma Hickman, (MD) February 2, 1893, (MG) G. M. Snider.

John Iva and Lizza Craig, (MD) December 7, 1892, (MG) P. O. Brant.

H. F. Newton and Jennie Snider, (MD) July, 1883, (MG) W. S. Bullock.

P. H. Brant and Nettie Richardson, (MD) 1893, (MG) P. O. Brant.

John Garrigns and Vene Richardson, (MD) July, 1893, (MG) W. W. Watkins.

Warren Webb and Minnie Bailey, (MD) December, 1896, (MG) H. Williams.

J. H. Hurley and Onie Turnbow, (MD) October 20, 1895 (MG) J. F. Montgomery.

W. L. Hurley and Ether Turnbow, (MD) August 15, 1896, (MG) D. F. Tarter.

D. N. Craig and Harriet Hickman, (MD) ?, (MG) J. F. Montgomery.

G. A. Price and Cora Shreve, (MD) December 24, 1894, (MG)

J. F. Montgomery.
Levi Wheeler and Cora Grinder, (MD) December 26, 1897, (MG) J. W. Breton.
J. E. Tackett and Mahata Clements, (MD) September, 1899, (MG) A. R. Jones.
S. C. Tackett and Netter Turnbow, (MD) September 24, 1899, (MG) G. S. Nelson.
A. H. Hurley and Dora Rowland, (MD) September 24, 1899, (MG) G. S. Nelson.

Register of Deaths

Name	Date
Jno. D. Shreve	June 11, 1892
Ann Richardson	February 26, 1893
Rinda (sic) Hamilton	August 29, 1893
Fanny Davis	May 11, 1894
Mary Craig	August 1, 1896
C. C. Turnbow	February 25, 1895
Vene Garrigns	November, 1896
Thomas Davis	In the Winter, 1895
Hugh Hamilton	---
W. H. Burns	Winter, 1897
Catherine Turnbow	Summer, 1895
Susan Pryor	1897
Clara Kyle	July, 1899

Register of Adult Baptisms

Name	Date	Reverend
Sarah E. Henkle	Jan., 1880	W. W. Watkins
John Hill	Jul., 1881	W. W. Watkins
A. H. Kyle	Sep., 1881	W. W. Watkins
Victoria E. Lemly	Sep., 1881	W. W. Watkins
Alex. Story	Oct., 1881	W. W. Watkins
J. P. Dollar	Jul., 1882	W. W. Watkins
Annie C. Dollar	Jul., 1882	W. W. Watkins
Ed Worton	Jul., 1882	W. W. Watkins
L. M. Cordale	Jul. 29, 1882	W. W. Watkins
Espheran Coffman	May 21, 1882	W. W. Watkins
John Hagleman	Mar. 26, 1882	W. W. Watkins
S. H. Bowland	Jul., 1881	W. W. Watkins
Ellen Bowlen	Jul., 1881	W. W. Watkins
W. G. Burns	Aug., 1882	W. W. Watkins
Wiley Burns	Aug., 1882	W. W. Watkins
Mrs. Louisa Burns	Aug., 1882	W. W. Watkins
Mary E. Churchill	Sep., 24, 1882	W. W. Watkins
R. M. Lemely	Oct. 15, 1882	W. W. Watkins
William Parton	May 20, 1882	W. W. Watkins
John Parton	May 20, 1882	W. W. Watkins
Margaret M. Lemly	Oct. 15, 1882	W. W. Watkins
Martin Snider	Aug. 19, 1883	J.F. Montgomery
Yennie (sic) Henkle	Aug. 26, 1883	J.F. Montgomery

Name	Date	Reverend
Silas E. Linton	Jul. 31, 1887	W. W. Watkins
Mattie Cordale	Jul. 31, 1887	W. W. Watkins
George Poe	Jul. 31, 1887	W. W. Watkins
Millie Petty	Jul. 31, 1887	W. W. Watkins
Charley Price	Sep. 4, 1892	Joe Smith
Richard M. Poe	Sep. 4, 1892	Joe Smith
Ellen Manvant	Sep. 4, 1892	Joe Smith
Leo Bullock	Sep. 4, 1892	Joe Smith
Sid Richardson	Sep. 4, 1892	Joe Smith
Corii Shrievey (?)	Sep. 4, 1892	Joe Smith
Jen Snider	Sep. 4, 1892	Joe Smith
Eliva Craig	Sep. 4, 1892	Joe Smith
Netie Richardson	Sep. 4, 1892	Joe Smith
Joseph Poe	Sep. 4, 1892	Joe Smith
James A. Poe	Sep. 4, 1892	Joe Smith
John Iva	Sep. 4, 1892	Joe Smith
Robert Newton	Sep. 4, 1892	Joe Smith
Ellar Poe	Sep. 4, 1892	Joe Smith
Nemy Hickman	Sep. 4, 1892	Joe Smith
Vene Richardson	Sep. 4, 1892	Joe Smith
Leiva Hickman	Sep. 4, 1892	Joe Smith
Lena Rowland	Sep. 4, 1892	Joe Smith
Wade Walters	Sep. 4, 1892	Joe Smith
Giles Richardson	Sep. 4, 1892	Joe Smith
John Shrieves	Sep. 4, 1892	Joe Smith
Wil Craig	Sep. 4, 1892	Joe Smith
Luther Berry	Sep. 4, 1892	Joe Smith
Henry Rowland	Sep. 4, 1892	Joe Smith
Elty (?) Craig	Sep. 4, 1892	Joe Smith
Jam. Beavis	Sep. 4, 1892	Joe Smith
George Ingram	Sep. 4, 1892	Joe Smith
Wm. Walker	Sep. 4, 1892	Joe Smith
Ja. Tucker	Sep. 4, 1892	Joe Smith
Nancy Hamilton	Sep. 4, 1892	Joe Smith
Ely Shrievey	Sep. 4, 1892	Joe Smith
Pall Lienalin (?)	Sep. 4, 1892	Joe Smith
Giney Herley	Sep. 4, 1892	Joe Smith
Dan Walker	Sep. 4, 1892	Joe Smith
Daria Smith	Aug. 31, 1893	Joe A. Smith
Ader Smith	Aug. 31, 1893	Joe A. Smith
Rowea Smith	Aug. 31, 1893	Joe A. Smith
Coria Pervis	Aug. 31, 1893	Joe A. Smith
Rovea Stevenison	Aug. 31, 1892	Joe A. Smith
Fannie Dennis	Aug. 31, 1892	Joe A. Smith
George Price	Sep. 5, 1894	W. W. Watkins
Netia Burns	Sep. 5, 1894	W. W. Watkins
Cnel. Smith	Sep. 5, 1894	W. W. Watkins
Alpha Moore	Sep. 5, 1894	W. W. Watkins

Name	Date	Reverend
Peter Pryor	Sep. 5, 1894	W. W. Watkins
Wil Hamilton	Sep. 5, 1894	W. W. Watkins
Mary Baley	Sep. 15, 1895	J. E. Montgomery
Ellen Garrigns	Sep. 15, 1895	J. E. Montgomery
Willie Leyman	Sep. 15, 1895	J. E. Montgomery
Emer Sirens	Sep. 15, 1895	J. E. Montgomery
Nety Turnbow	Sep. 15, 1895	J. E. Montgomery
Miny Baley	Sep. 15, 1895	J. E. Montgomery
Ether Herley	Sep. 15, 1895	J. E. Montgomery
Anie Kinslo	Sep. 15, 1895	J. E. Montgomery
Eler Craig	Sep. 15, 1895	J. E. Montgomery
Doria Rolan	Sep. 15, 1895	J. E. Montgomery
Waid Watkins	Sep. 15, 1895	W. W. Watkins
William Herty	Feb. 16, 1896	J. F. Montgomery
Sandra Hurley	Feb. 16, 1896	J. F. Montgomery
Noria Grinder	Sep. 9, 1896	J. F. Montgomery
Georgia Grinder	Sep. 9, 1896	J. F. Montgomery
Clari Kyle	Oct. 20, 1896	J. F. Montgomery
Ella Brant	Oct. 20, 1896	J. F. Montgomery
Maria Brant	Oct. 20, 1896	J. F. Montgomery
Rena Walters	Sep. 2, 1897	J. W. Bruton
J. E. Tackett	Aug. 2, 1899	Joe A. Smith
L. J. Wheeler	Aug. 2, 1899	Joe A. Smith
Ora Grinder	Aug. 2, 1899	Joe A. Smith
Lonie Bradford	Aug. 2, 1899	Joe A. Smith
G. W. Eubanks	Aug. 2, 1899	Joe A. Smith
Henry Eubanks	Aug. 2, 1899	Joe A. Smith
Annie Eubanks	Aug. 2, 1899	Joe A. Smith
Dora Trigg	Aug. 2, 1899	Joe A. Smith

Register of Communicants

Name	Comments
F. M. Lemley	Adm. May, 1881, Dis. Dec., 1890
Caroline Lemley	Adm. May, 1881, Dis. Dec., 1890
Ephraim Hill	Adm. May, 1881, Dis. Feb., 1889
Susan Hill	Adm. May, 1881, Dis. Feb., 1889
Samuel H. Bowland	Adm. May, 1881, Dis. Feb., 1889
J. M. Holleybaugh	Adm. May, 1881, Dis. Feb., 1889
Mary J. Holleybaugh	Adm. May, 1881, Dis. Feb., 1889
Elizabeth Linton	Adm. May, 1881, Dis. Dec. 20, 1890
G. L. Lemley	Adm. May, 1881, Dis. Dec. 20, 1890
Jane Lemley	Adm. May, 1881, Dis. Dec. 20, 1890
J. L. Tyler	Adm. May, 1881, Dis. Dec. 20, 1890
Harriet Dixon	Adm. May, 1881, Dis. Dec. 20, 1890

Name	Comments
Abitha Coffman	Adm. May, 1881, Dis. Dec. 20, 1890
Rebecca Coffman	Adm. May, 1881, Dis. Dec. 20, 1890
Susan Sinclair	Adm. May, 1881, d. July, 1885
William Petty	Adm. May, 1881 Dis. Dec. 20, 1890
Elizabeth Petty	Adm. May, 1881, d. Aug. 13, 1882
J. T. Churchill	Adm. May, 1881, Dis. Dec. 20, 1890
J. M. Henkle	Adm. May, 1881, Dis. Feb., 1889
Sarah A. Henkle	Adm. May, 1881, Dis. Feb., 1889
Sarah C. Henkle	Adm. Jan., 1881, Dis. Feb., 1889
Rachel Petty	Adm. Mar., 1880, d. Aug., 1887
John Hill	Adm. Jul., 1881, Dis. Dec., 1890
A. H. Kyle	Adm. Sep., 1881, Dis. Feb., 1889
Victoria Lemley	Adm. Sep., 1881
Alx. Story	Adm. Oct., 1881, Dis. Jul. 23, 1884
Manery Bennett	Adm. May, 1881, Dis. Dec., 1890
Wm. F. Rose	Adm. Sep. 15, 1881, Joined the Baptist, 1885
Mary Rose	Adm. Sep. 18, 1881, Dis. 1885
S. H. Bowland	Adm. Sep. 18, 1881, Dis. Dec., 1890
Ellen Bowland	Adm. Sep. 18, 1881, Dis. Dec., 1890
Oliver F. Leach	Adm. May 21, 1882, Dis. Dec., 1890
Mary Leach	Adm. May 21, 1882, Dis. Dec., 1890
Esperan Coffman	Adm. May 21, 1882, Dis. Dec., 1890
J. P. Dollar	d. Apr., 1884
Ann E. Dollar	Dis. Dec., 1890
E. B. Wooten	Dis. 1883
H. S. Kinslow	Dis. Aug., 1886
Haney Kinslow	Dis. Aug., 1886
M. C. Dollar	Dis. Dec., 1890
Sallie A. Dollar	Dis. Dec., 1890
L. M. Cordale	Adm. Jul. 29, 1882, Dis. Dec., 1890
J. K. Sinclair	Adm. Jul. 30, 1882, Dis. 1885
Mary G. Sinclair	Dis. Dec., 1890
W. H. Parten	Adm. Aug. 2, 1882, Sus. 1887
W. J. Burns	Adm. Aug. 20, 1882, d. 1884
John Hagleman	---

Name	Comments
Wiley Burns	Adm. Aug. 20, 1882, Dis. Dec., 1890
Sister Louisa Burns	Adm. Aug. 20, 1882, Dis. Dec., 1890
Polly A. Story	Dis. Jul., 23, 1884, Returned 1886
Mary E. Churchill	d. Mar., 1888
R. M. Lemley	Dis. 1890
Margaret Lemley	Dis. 1890
Samuel Crow	---
James Burns	Adm. Aug., 1882, d. 1886
Martin Synder	Adm. Aug., 1883, Sus. Jul. 17, 1885, Restored Jun., 1887
John Partain	Adm. May, 1883, Dis. Aug., 1880
Samuel Burton	Adm. May, 1883, Sus. May, 1887, Joined the Methodists
Martha Churchill	Adm. Aug., 1883, Dis. Dec., 1890
Tennie Henkle	Adm. Aug., 1883, Dis. Feb., 1889
M. E. Coffman	Adm. Sep., 1885, Dis. Dec., 1890
T. M. Poe	Adm. Jun., 1885, Dis. Dec., 1890
Elizabeth Poe	Adm. Jun., 1885, Dis. Dec., 1890
Alice Poe	Adm. Jun., 1885, Dis. Dec., 1890
Silas E. Linton	Adm. Jul., 1887, Dis. Dec., 1890
George Poe	Adm. Jul., 1887, Dis. Dec., 1890
B. F. Sinclair	Adm. Jul., 1887, Dis. Dec., 1890
Eliza Sinclair	Adm. Jul., 1887, Dis. Dec., 1890
Mattie Petty	Adm. Jul., 1887, Dis. Dec., 1890
Lulu Leach	Adm. Sep., 1887, Dis. Dec., 1890
Belle Hill	Adm. Sep., 1887, Dis. Feb., 1889
H. L. Stafford	Adm. Oct., 1887, Sus. Jan., 1889
Mattie Cordale	Adm. Oct., 1887, Dis. Dec., 1890

Silver Creek Cumberland Presbyterian Church, Silver Creek Maury County, Tennessee.

Register of Black Members

As follows: Pry Bowden, Elizor Bowden, Lucinda Cochran, Rachel Hill, Emeline McFall, Manervia McFall.

Register of Membership

As follows: Mary Scott, Sarah Freeland, Martha Freeland, Nancy Freeland, Nancy Alred, Parthenia Denton, James Hughs, Francis Vaughn, James E. Hill, Martha A. Casley, Parratha Lancaster, Sarah A. Hughs, Jane Casley, Adaline Vaughn, James Freeland, John B. Freeland, Jane M. E. Holland, Edward M. Smith, George Moore, Sarah Moore, A. J. Holland, Burwell Canon, James D. Hill, William Bowden, Mary S. Bowden, Arthur W. Smith, Ann B. Smith, Robert C. Bowden, Nancy Hill, Sophia A. Holland, John L. Smith, Robert Casley, Caroline Casley, Calvin Carrigon, Sarah Carrigon, Oliva Canon, Nelson Davis,

Margaret C. Freeland, Dovy F. Cochran, Lucinda Scott, Joseph M. Craig, Nancy M. Craig, Rachel Craig, Margret Ballard, Malissa Bay, Francis Bay, Larken Bay, Martha M. White, Aaron Cheek, James P. White, John Craig, Sarah Craig, Mary A. White, Robert B. White, Joseph R. Freeland, Green Freeland, Mary D. Bowden, Powhattan Freeland, James Freeland, Matilda Craig, James A. Casley, Emely Loftin, M. L. E. Denham, John Lamar, Mary Lamar, Tidelia A. Fanett, John T. Casley, Benjamin L. Cocklet, William Peek, William l. Casley, ELizabeth A. Casley, John A. T. Scribner, Mary U. Freeland, John T. Freeland, Sarah E. Hill, Mary Freeland, Hartwell Pucket.

Register of Infant Baptisms

Marion Bowden, (PRTS) Wm. and Mary S. Bowden, (BD) May 27, 1844.

Cynthia C. Holland, (PRTS) A. J. H. and Sophia A. Holland, (BD) August 24, 1845.

Winefred S. Holland, (PRTS) A. J. H. and Sophia A. Holland, (BD) August 24, 1845.

William J. Holland, (PRTS) A. J. H. and Sophia A. Holland, (BD) August 24, 1845.

Tyre L. Holland, (PRTS) A. J. H. and Sophia A. Holland, (BD) August 24, 1845.

Register of Marriages

Miss J. E. M. Smith and Smith (sic) M. Holland, (MD) September 12, 1843, (JP) Benomy Graham.

Register of Adult Baptisms

Name	Date
Calvin Carrigan	November 14, 1842
Sarah Carrigan	November 14, 1842
James Freeland	November, 1842
Lucinda Scott	November, 1842
Pleasant Holland (colored)	November 14, 1842
--y Bowden (colored)	November 14, 1842
Eliza Bowden (colored)	October 14, 1842
--aline Vaughn	October 14, 1842
---inda Cochran (colored)	October 14, 1842
James Hughs	August 24, 1845
Martha J. Casley	August 24, 1845
Francis Vaughn	August 24, 1845
----a Hill	August 24, 1845
----n McFall	August 24, 1845
Minirva McFall	August 24, 1845
George More	October 25, 1846
Sarah More	October 25, 1846
Parratha Lancaster	September 2, 1845
Green Freeland	July 9, 1848
Powhattan Freeland	July 9, 1848

Register of Births

Robert C. Bowden, (b.) December 14, 1842, (PRTS) Robert C.

and Mary Bowden.
   Marion Bowden, (b.) September 16, 1843, (PRTS) William and Mary S. Bowden.
   Lucinda Jane Carrigan, (b.) March 30, 1843, (PRTS) Calvin and Sarah Carrigan.
   Burwell Henderson Casley, (b.) April 12, 1843, (PRTS) Robert and Jane Casley.

Members Admitted, October 17, 1843
Burwell Canan, Jane E. M. Smith, Edward M. Smith, Mary Scott, Sarah Freeland, Nancy Freeland, Martha Freeland, Nancy Alred.

Members Anmitted, August 24, 1845
Francis Vaughn, James Hughs, James Hill, Martha J. Casky, Linda Hill (colored), Emiline McFall (colored), Mariah Whitaker, Manurvia McFall (colored)

Members Admitted, October 8, 1846
Nelson Davis, James Freeland, James E. M. Holland.

Members Admitted, July 25, 1847
James D. Freeland, Joseph F. Freeland, Mary D. Bowden, James B. Hill.

Members Admitted, November 14, 1847
Joseph M. Craig, Nancy Craig, Rachel Craig, Margaret Ballard, Malissa Box, Frances Box, Larkin Box, Marsha M. White, James P. White, John Craig, Sarah Craig, Mary A. White, Robt. B. White.

Members Dismissed, November 14, 1847
Arthur W. Smith, Ann B. Smith, John L. Smith.

Register of Deaths

Name	Date
Parathera Lancaster	June 24, 1848
Margret Ballard	March 7, 1849
Nancy Alred	September 4, 1853
Sarah E. Hill	June 15, 1854

Jacksonville Union Chapel, Jacksonville, Randolph County, Missouri.

Register of Pasters

Name	Ordained
F. Z. Shearon	April 3, 1898
R. S. Maupin	May 7, 1899

Register of Elders

Name	Ordained
Martin C. Adams	February 27, 1898
John A. Adams	February 27, 1898

Register of Communicants, February 27, 1898
C. H. Johnston, Lutharia F. Johnston, John M. Johnston, Allen J. Hines, Susan J. Hines, David G. Hines, George A. Hines, Henry M. Hines, Susie Hines, John A. Hines, Joseph S. Adams, Martin C. Adams, Ann Mary Adams, Mattie T. Adams, Ida

M. Adams, John A. Adams, Sallie Adams, Guite B. Hudson, Fannie Henderson, Sallie Johnson, Vina D. Garner, Daisy Garner, Amelia C. McCully, Henry M. Poers, A. B. Burton, Tula Gray, Margarite E. Terry, Elijah M. Terry, Mary F. Travis, Francis P. Brown, George F. Powers

SURNAME INDEX

---GHAM, 91
---LLER, 68
ADAIR, 6 10
ADAMS, 32-34 82 100 101
ADDINGTON, 49 51 53-55 58 59
AGNEW, 84
AKIN, 85 86
ALEXANDER, 82 83
ALFRED, 15
ALISON, 17
ALLEN, 6 50 51
ALLFRED, 43
ALLISON, 17
ALLREAD, 43 47
ALLRED, 42-45 47-49 90 91
ALRED, 45 46 49 98 100
ALRIDGE, 73
ALVERSON, 32 33
ALXANDER, 82
ANDERSON, 39 66 82 87
ANDREW, 3 12
ANGLE, 80
APPLE, 70 72-74 76
ARMSTRONG, 24 25 92
ARNOLD, 6
ASKEW, 6 77-79
ATCHERSON, 37
ATCHISON, 9
ATWELL, 64
AUSTEN, 42
AUSTIN, 75 76
AUTREE, 74 76
AUTREY, 76-78
AUTRIE, 73
AUTRY, 75 76
B----ON, 86
BACON, 17 56
BAILEY, 2-4 6 10-13 93
BAIN, 20
BAIRD, 38 39
BAITS, 14
BAKER, 4 11 32 34 80 81 88
BALEY, 92 96
BALL, 12 36
BALLARD, 99 100
BANDENBY, 19
BARKER, 3 4 6 7 12
BARNHART, 49-51 53-58
BARR, 84
BARRAGAR, 2
BARRAGER, 10

BATES, 14
BATTS, 82
BAWCUM, 85 87
BAY, 99
BEASLEY, 60 72 74
BEATY, 4 5
BEAVIS, 95
BECK, 71
BELK, 17
BELL, 26 61 71 72 90-92
BELTON, 88
BEMIS, 2 10
BENNETT, 80 97
BENNZETTE, 6
BERGER, 6
BERRY, 92 95
BIBERRY, 46
BIBY, 17
BIDDLECOME, 60
BIERHAUSE, 60
BIERHOUSE, 61
BILARY, 47
BILBARY, 47
BILBERRY, 45
BILBERY, 46
BILBREY, 45 46 48
BILLICK, 59
BIRAM, 92
BIRDWELL, 77
BLACK, 19-22 91 92
BLAKE, 40
BLAKELY, 22
BLANKET, 87
BLEDSOE, 15 16
BLEIL, 6
BLEVIN, 79
BLOOMER, 88
BLOUNT, 87 88
BOGARD, 68
BOHANAN, 85
BOILDON, 92
BOLING, 2 9
BOLTZER, 88
BOMAN, 45 46 48
BOND, 2 10
BOOFER, 16
BOONE, 6
BORDEN, 23
BOSTON, 36
BOSWELL, 36 42-46 48 49
BOULDIN, 36

BOULDING, 31 35
BOWDEN, 98-100
BOWERS, 53
BOWLAND, 94 96 97
BOWLEN, 94
BOWMAN, 50 54 56
BOX, 40 85 86 100
BRADFORD, 96
BRADLEY, 4 13 82 83 91
BRADNEY, 19
BRADSHAW, 3 12
BRANAN, 90
BRANARD, 55
BRANCH, 40 41
BRANDENBERG, 23
BRANDENBURG, 21-23
BRANNUM, 5
BRANSON, 19
BRANT, 93 96
BREATES, 20
BRECK, 61
BRETON, 94
BREUSCH, 34
BRIGGANCE, 85 86
BROCK, 32
BRONAUGH, 9 13
BROOK, 25 26
BROOKS, 8 24 25 31
BROTHER, 6
BROUAGH, 5
BROWN, 1 6 8 16 17 42 46 49-
  52 54 56 57 59 60 70 74 82
  88 90-92 101
BROWNE, 80
BROWNING, 24 26-29 51 58
BROYLES, 59
BROZLES, 55
BRUNK, 22
BRUSH, 34
BRUTON, 96
BRYANCOR, 61
BRYSON, 6
BUCHANAN, 19 20 22 23 25 32
  33
BUCHANNAN, 23
BUCK, 52
BULER, 87
BULLOCK, 79 80 93 95
BUNCH, 21
BURCH, 68
BURGES, 8
BURGESS, 1
BURGSTRESSER, 18
BURGSTRESSOR, 19
BURGSTUSSER, 19
BURNS, 38 53 92-95 97 98
BURTON, 69 70 71 73-75 79 81
  98 101
BUSH, 73

BUSHING, 93
BUSHON, 50
BUSHONG, 56
BUTLER, 6
BUTT, 81
BYME, 71
BYRN, 83
BYRNE, 74 75
BYRON, 82
CAHAM, 83
CAIN, 16
CALDWELL, 6 7 24 25 27 29 62
  87 88
CALDWILL, 30
CALE, 2 10
CALHOUN, 36 83
CALLETT, 85
CALVERT, 34
CAMBELL, 14
CAMERON, 12
CAMPBELL, 14 20 21 25 49-51
  54-56 58 60 62 81
CANAN, 100
CANBY, 60 62
CANN, 20 21
CANON, 98
CANTREL, 42 45
CANTRELL, 42-45 47 48
CANTRILL, 46 48
CARA, 16
CARL, 20
CARLOCK, 13-17 72 76
CARLSON, 13
CARNAHAN, 19 21 23
CARNEY, 18
CARNSON, 20
CARPENTER, 6
CARR, 16 43 47 62
CARRIGAN, 99 100
CARRIGON, 98
CARTEN, 71
CARTER, 6 60 71 74 79-81 91
CASEY, 2-7 9 11 12
CASKY, 100
CASLEY, 98-100
CASSADY, 26
CASSY, 1
CAYWOOD, 62
CEICIL, 6
CELL, 61 62
CHANEY, 82
CHAPMAN, 33 39
CHASE, 61
CHEEK, 40 41 61 99
CHENOWETH, 92
CHILES, 67
CHINEWORTH, 91
CHOATE, 83
CHURCHILL, 94 97 98

CLAGETT, 1 8
CLAMROCK, 35
CLARK, 10 13 25 27-29 39 50 51 57 59 72 74
CLEMENTS, 94
CLEVENGER, 58
CLODFELTER, 49 50 56 57
COCHRAN, 38 98 99
COCKLET, 99
COCKRILL, 40 41
COFFMAN, 94 97 98
COLE, 6 22
COLEMAN, 14-17 62
COLLETT, 86
COLLETTE, 85 86
COLLIER, 77 90-92
COLLINGS, 36
COLLINS, 23
COMER, 2 6 10 12 13
COMMER, 10
COOK, 2 10 20 43 44 47 62 88 89
COOPER, 15 42 70 90 92
COORLANE, 54
COPELAND, 13 15-17 46
COPLAN, 46
COPLAND, 44
COPLIN, 82 83
COPPAGE, 6
CORBAN, 25
CORDALE, 94 95 97 98
CORDER, 24 25 30 31
CORETALL, 92
CORNWELL, 76-79
COUPER, 15
COVINGTON, 6 77 78
COWAN, 75 76
COWARD, 91 92
COWPER, 15
COX, 15 16 34 60 61 84-87 91 92
CRABTREE, 1 7 36 39
CRAGE, 44
CRAIG, 15 40 41 51 92-96 99 100
CRANE, 59
CRASFORD, 19
CRAVEN, 17-19
CRAVENS, 15
CRAWFORD, 15-17 20-23
CRAY, 48
CRESSY, 6
CRIM, 24-28 30 31
CROCKETT, 53
CROFFORD, 15
CROFORD, 15
CROOKS, 1 3-7 9 11 13
CROSIER, 21
CROSS, 49 54

CROTHER, 62
CROW, 11 98
CROWFORD, 16 91
CROZIER, 20
CRUM, 23
CRUZ, 23
CULBERTSON, 25 31
CULLAM, 16
CULLEY, 6
CULLOM, 16
CULP, 80 81
CUNNINGHAM, 20 22 32
CURTIS, 6
DACOMB, 4
DALRYMPLE, 92
DALTON, 25 27 28
DANFORTH, 57
DANN, 90
DARLING, 4
DARWIN, 79
DAULTON, 25 30 31
DAVIDSON, 66
DAVIS, 4 8 37 38 42-45 50 56 62 63 81 94 98 100
DEAN, 49 55 57 59
DEASON, 85 86
DEFRATES, 63
DEHAVEN, 77
DEMPSEY, 66 67
DENHAM, 99
DENNIE, 75
DENNIS, 95
DENTON, 98
DERR, 62
DESCOMBS, 3 6 9 11 13
DESKIN, 34
DESKINS, 33 34
DEVALL, 24
DEVORE, 33
DIAL, 15
DICKEN, 74
DILLARD, 15 70-74
DILLINER, 26
DIRNEL, 52
DISERT, 32
DISHMAN, 42 45
DISHMON, 44 45 48
DITTY, 79
DIVEN, 22
DIXON, 40 72 74 96
DOBENS, 90
DOLLAR, 94 97
DOLTON, 27
DORY, 67
DOWLEN, 90 91
DOWLIN, 90 91
DOWNESS, 36
DRAKE, 40
DRAPER, 78

DRAUGHN, 71
DRESHEE, 26
DUCKWORTH, 67
DUKE, 75
DUNAWAY, 11 13
DUNCAN, 55 56 81 92
DUNHAM, 51
DUNLAP, 59 79-81
DUNN, 3 11
DUNWOODY, 51 58
DURHAM, 58
DURVIN, 22
DUTTEN, 34
DUVALL, 24
DYCUS, 77
DYER, 20
EAGER, 4 9
EAGLESON, 2 4 5 8-10
EALAM, 64
EALEM, 61
EARLE, 20 21 22
EASTRIDGE, 51 52 54-56 58 59
EATON, 81
EBBERTING, 69
EDDINGTON, 52
EDINGTON, 91 92
EDMINSTON, 20
EDMISTON, 20 22 23
EDMONDS, 31
EDMUNDS, 25 30
EDWARDS, 22 59
EGNEW, 84
ELDER, 8 14 15 61 70 74 87
ELDREG, 49
ELDRIDGE, 16 17
ELINA, 36
ELISTON, 66
ELLEN, 70
ELLER, 74 75
ELLIOTT, 2 3 5 8 9 11 13 64
ELLIS, 92
ELRED, 45
ELROD, 72
ELTHEL, 9
ELY, 7
EMBREY, 6
EMERY, 25 31
ESKERN, 7
ESRA, 32
ESRY, 32-35
EUBANKS, 93 96
EVANS, 4 11 16 21 77
EZELLE, 21 22
FALES, 88
FANETT, 99
FAR, 90
FARLEY, 17
FARLON, 84
FARLOW, 85 86

FARR, 6
FAUBIAN, 25 26
FAVERS, 38
FENCH, 44
FENLEY, 12
FEREL, 6
FERGUSON, 53 55
FERRAL, 15 16
FERREL, 71 78
FERRELL, 17 70 71 74-79
FERRIL, 13 15 16
FERRILL, 15-17
FERSLING, 16
FIELAND, 6
FIELDEN, 8
FIELDS, 39 83
FIKE, 67
FILE, 88
FILLIPS, 42 43
FINGLE, 6
FINKS, 66
FIRMAN, 25
FISHER, 69 86 88
FITTS, 38
FITZWATER, 5 6 7
FLOYDS, 22
FLY, 2
FLYNT, 35 36
FOLLETT, 23
FORD, 11 12
FORMAN, 24 26-29
FOSKET, 53
FOSTER, 6
FOX, 91
FRAME, 64 87 88
FRANKLIN, 36 75
FRANKS, 86
FRASELL, 60
FRAZER, 34
FRAZIER, 32-34 86
FREELAND, 6 98-100
FREEZE, 36
FRELDEN, 1
FRENCH, 42 43 45 46 48 49
FROGG, 26
FRY, 86
FURGESON, 53
GAINES, 65 69
GAINS, 3 13 53
GALBRAITH, 66
GANS, 64
GARNER, 91 92 101
GARRET, 15
GARRETT, 82
GARRIGNS, 93 94 96
GARST, 49 52 54 57 59
GARTH, 6
GASKELL, 69
GASSETT, 86

106

GASTON, 90
GEELE, 51
GENTRY, 25
GERMAN, 17
GIBSON, 34 38
GIFFORD, 22
GILBERT, 6
GILENTINE, 16
GILLAM, 6 7 40 65 66
GILLESPIE, 36
GILLIAM, 66
GILLINGHAM, 17
GILLINTINE, 17
GIVENS, 32
GLASGOW, 1 7-9
GODARD, 22 23
GODDARD, 21
GOINGS, 7
GOLDSMITH, 6
GOOD, 49 52-60
GOODING, 34
GOODPASTURE, 71
GOODWIN, 37 38 40 50 51 57-59
GOOLSBY, 73 75 76 78
GOOSE, 52
GOSSETT, 86
GOWENS, 1
GOWINGS, 34
GRAFFORD, 28 30
GRAHAM, 99
GRAVES, 35
GRAY, 76 101
GREEN, 74
GREY, 1 5-7 88
GRIDER, 44 47
GRIFFIN, 25 29 30 35 36
GRINDER, 92 94 96
GRISHAM, 69-79
GRISSOM, 70 79
GRONAMIAH, 84 85
GRONER, 90-92
GUIAN, 1
GUILFORD, 16
GUINN, 25
GUION, 2 6 9 10
GUTHERY, 87 88
HAGAR, 16
HAGEMAN, 61 64
HAGEN, 69
HAGER, 15
HAGLEMAN, 94 97
HAINER, 31
HAINES, 23
HAINS, 56
HAISER, 26
HALE, 52 56 58
HALES, 50
HALL, 52 53 59 60 90
HAMBRICK, 41

HAMILTON, 87 92 94-96
HAMMAR, 12
HAMMES, 26
HAMMETT, 17-19
HAMMOCK, 45 48
HAMMON, 68
HAMMOND, 68
HAMMONS, 10 11
HAMNER, 31
HANCOCK, 85 86
HAND, 6
HANKINS, 10
HANKS, 22
HANNAN, 50 51 55
HANNON, 51 58
HANSFORD, 38 39
HAPPERS, 64
HARDISTER, 32
HARDY, 21-23
HARGIS, 69-71 73-79
HARIS, 77 79
HARMAN, 81
HARPER, 91
HARRIGER, 6
HARRIS, 20 26 30-35 50 56 57
    73 74 76 84 85 87
HARRISON, 17 20-22 52
HARTLEY, 19
HARTMAN, 17 19
HARWARD, 13
HARWOOD, 6
HATHAWAY, 4 13
HATTAWAY, 13
HATTON, 36
HAVENS, 66
HAWKINS, 2 93
HAY, 36 52 53
HAYDEN, 24-31
HAYNES, 32
HAYS, 1 4 7 49-52 57-60
HAYSLER, 6
HAYTER, 13-17 87 88
HEAND, 32
HECKTER, 3 12
HECTOR, 12 88
HELM, 6 7
HELMAN, 54 56
HENDERSON, 20-22 40 64 101
HENDRIX, 36
HENKLE, 92 94 97 98
HENSON, 19
HERINGTON, 92
HERKETT, 6
HERLEY, 95 96
HERRON, 52
HERTY, 96
HICKERSON, 1 8 9
HICKINSON, 1
HICKLEN, 88

HICKMAN, 93 95
HICKS, 3 11 12 38
HILL, 15 38 43-45 48 88 92 94 96-100
HINCHER, 3 11
HINDS, 20 21 23
HINES, 100
HINKLE, 1 2 9
HINTON, 1 4-7 12
HISKETT, 18
HITCH, 25
HITES, 14
HOGAN, 70
HOLDMAN, 36
HOLEFIELD, 82
HOLIFIELD, 83
HOLLAND, 98-100
HOLLEMAN, 70-76 78
HOLLEYBAUGH, 96
HOLLYBAUGH, 92
HOLMES, 70-72 74 82 83
HOLT, 2 6 10
HOLTON, 12
HOMES, 15
HOOD, 2 10
HOOVER, 32 68 69
HORN, 25 28 52 55
HORNBACK, 69
HORNBECK, 65 66
HOSA, 35
HOTCHKISS, 25
HOUSER, 92
HOUX, 2
HOWARD, 14 15 17 18
HOWEL, 27
HOWELL, 28
HOWLETT, 59
HUBBARD, 1
HUDSON, 101
HUFF, 6 73 74 78 79
HUFFINES, 43
HUGHES, 9 50 51
HUGHS, 52 56 59 98-100
HULL, 15 59
HUMBLE, 25 30 31 80
HUMPHREY, 39
HUNDS, 19
HUNT, 13 15 16
HUNTER, 28
HURLEY, 93 94 96
HUSDON, 52
HUTTON, 65 66
IGLEHART, 38
INGRAM, 95
IRISH, 92
IRVIN, 16 87
IRWIN, 66 88 89
ISRAEL, 92
IVA, 93 95

IYRE, 20
JACK, 17-19
JACKOBY, 33 34
JACKSON, 14 15 37
JACOBY, 33
JAMES, 22 31
JAYNE, 88
JAYNES, 88
JEMISON, 68
JENINGS, 91 92
JENKINS, 31-33
JENNINGS, 91 92
JHONSON, 49
JOB, 23
JOHNSON, 6 8 14-16 37 45 50 56 57 64 68 90 92 93 101
JOHNSTON, 14 15 20 36 100
JONES, 2 9 15-17 24 25 35 49 53-55 82 83 94
JUDGE, 6
JULIEN, 90
JUNKER, 33
KEASLING, 91
KEELE, 58
KEILSING, 17
KEILSLING, 16
KEISLING, 16 17
KELAN, 83
KELAND, 83
KELLER, 81
KELLEY, 21 80
KELLY, 20 22 81
KELVEY, 40
KEMP, 6
KENSINGER, 3-5 9 11
KERNELL, 91 92
KERRICK, 38 39
KEY, 79-81
KIDWELL, 35
KIELSING, 17
KIESLING, 16
KIMBROUGH, 68
KIMSAY, 6
KIMSEY, 1 4 6 7
KING, 4 50 51 57 72 75 76
KINGSBERRY, 9
KINSINGER, 10 12
KINSLO, 96
KINSLOW, 97
KINSLOY, 93
KIRK, 85 86
KIRKPATRICK, 18 19
KISER, 29 31
KNIGHT, 76
KNOX, 24 29 92
KOGER, 16 17
KRIBS, 32
KRUSE, 60 61 64
KYLE, 94 96 97

LACE, 14
LACKARD, 53
LAMAN, 64
LAMAR, 6 99
LAMBERT, 6 8
LAMROCK, 84-86
LANCASTER, 98-100
LAND, 6 9
LANDEN, 14
LANDON, 13
LANE, 52
LANSDEN, 13 14
LANSDON, 13 14
LANUM, 39
LASHBROOK, 38 39
LAW, 17
LAWLIS, 73
LAWSON, 54 56 57
LAWTON, 36
LAYCOCK, 11 13
LEA, 15 17 92
LEACH, 97 98
LEAR, 24-26 29 31
LEDBETER, 42 44 45 49
LEDBETTER, 14-17 43 46 48
LEDFORD, 15 17
LEE, 14 27 37 40 55 68 71-74 76
LEIGHTON, 25
LEMAN, 15
LEMELY, 94
LEMLEY, 96-98
LEMLY, 94
LEMMINS, 14
LEMMONS, 14
LENAMAN, 16
LENLEZ, 92
LEWIS, 4 6 13
LEYMAN, 96
LIENALIN, 95
LINDER, 15 16 46
LINDSEY, 6
LINDSLEG, 54
LINDSLEY, 54
LINSTONE, 9
LINTON, 95 96 98
LITERAL, 22 23
LITTLE, 39 40
LITTRELL, 1 2
LIVINGSTON, 15
LOFLIN, 22
LOFTIN, 99
LONES, 90 91
LONFORD, 20
LOOPER, 42 45 46 49
LOUES, 87
LOUIS, 71 89
LOVE, 17 91
LOWRANCE, 24 60

LOWRY, 18 19
LOYD, 6
LUCK, 23
LUCY, 92
LUIN, 15
LUNDAY, 75
LUTZ, 53 60
LYCOOK, 3
LYNCH, 16
M'CLARNOCK, 35
M'DONALD, 13
M'KY, 14
M'MILLAN, 14
M'MILLION, 51
MABRY, 72
MACKEY, 36
MADDOCK, 87
MADDUX, 69 73-79
MAIN, 11
MAIZE, 1 2 4 5 7 8
MAIZO, 10
MALIN, 86
MALLICOAT, 21
MALONE, 17 18 91
MANEAR, 71 72
MANGUM, 91
MANIER, 73
MANN, 54
MANNING, 17 19 32
MANNS, 19 59
MANVANT, 95
MARCUM, 36
MARGESON, 3 4
MARK, 39
MARRS, 21-23 53
MARSHALL, 91 92
MARTAIN, 42-44
MARTIN, 14-17 38 50 57 59 82 83 87
MARY, 82
MASON, 6
MASSEY, 86
MASTON, 24 28
MATHENY, 42
MATHERLY, 53
MATHES, 66
MATHEWS, 60
MATT, 71
MATTHEWS, 54 60
MATTOX, 89
MAUPIN, 100
MAXWELL, 24 31
MAY, 85
MAYBERRY, 22
MAYNARD, 76 78 79
MAYS, 1 83 92
MAZE, 1
MCADAMS, 53 54
MCALRAVY, 49

MCCALL, 1 8
MCCANN, 2 4 6 9 10
MCCLELLAN, 70
MCCLOUD, 25 27
MCCOLLINS, 6
MCCORD, 60
MCCORMICK, 20
MCCOUN, 65
MCCOWEN, 69
MCCOWN, 66 67
MCCOY, 63
MCCULLANAH, 32
MCCULLOUGH, 32-34
MCCULLY, 101
MCDEARMAN, 74
MCDONALD, 16 17 69-75 79
MCDONNEL, 69 79
MCDONNOL, 14
MCDONNOLD, 13-16
MCDORMAN, 12
MCELLWAIN, 86
MCELROY, 92
MCELVAIN, 1
MCFALL, 98-100
MCFARLAND, 6 50 51 57
MCFORTUNE, 31
MCGARHEE, 36
MCGEHEE, 63
MCGLOTHLEN, 89
MCGLOTHLIN, 88
MCHOYT, 38
MCILLWAIN, 84-86
MCILRAVY, 59
MCILRAVZ, 50
MCILROY, 55
MCINTIRE, 26 27 31
MCINTRE, 25
MCINTYE, 25
MCINTYRE, 29 31
MCKINLEY, 69-74 76 79
MCKINNIE, 75
MCKINSEY, 67
MCKLANE, 1
MCLAIN, 91
MCLATHLUE, 87
MCLAUGHLIN, 17 18
MCLAUHLIN, 18
MCLEOD, 59
MCLOED, 50
MCMAHAN, 7
MCNEAL, 49-51 53-55 57
MCNEILL, 60 61 63
MCPHERSON, 17 18 22
MCPHILLON, 63
MCQUITTEN, 11
MCRENNOLDS, 91
MCSULLIVAN, 84
MEANS, 14
MEDCALF, 89

MELOND, 27
MELTON, 67 83
MERCER, 66
MERDOCK, 15
MERRILL, 64
METCALF, 88
MEYERS, 15
MICKLES, 87
MICKLSON, 67
MILES, 40 41
MILLAKEN, 89
MILLER, 6 9 32-34 47 55 65-68
    77 86 88
MILLNER, 63
MILLS, 2 9 67
MILOAD, 25
MILTON, 14
MITCHEL, 22 54 73 88
MITCHELL, 26 30 76 89
MOAD, 1
MONTGOMERY, 93 94 96
MOOR, 54
MOORE, 1-4 6-12 50 51 58 63
    68 91 95
MOOREN, 55
MOORLAND, 54
MOOSE, 37
MORE, 99
MOREDOCK, 15
MORGAN, 49 50 52 54-60 72
MORGART, 4 10 13
MORGIN, 72
MORNYRE, 61
MORRIS, 10 34 85 86
MORRISON, 21
MORROW, 52 54
MORTON, 21 23 57
MOSBY, 23
MOSELEY, 40
MOSELY, 39 85 87
MOSLEY, 36-39
MOSS, 23-29 31 43 45
MOWERY, 63 64
MULLENS, 82
MULLINS, 17
MUNKER, 88
MUNKERS, 87
MURPHEY, 4 41
MURPHY, 5
MURRAY, 3 4 6 7 11 92
MURRY, 91
MUTHENY, 43
MYERS, 71 73
MYRES, 70 73-75 79
NAFF, 91
NAIL, 20
NASH, 10
NCILROY, 53
NEAL, 4 23

NEALS, 23
NEALY, 16 17
NEBLY, 16
NEELEY, 15
NEELY, 16
NEIL, 6 57
NELBY, 16
NELSON, 92 94
NEUMINSTER, 55
NEWBERG, 16
NEWLAND, 19
NEWLEY, 17
NEWMAN, 52
NEWSOM, 84-87
NEWTON, 93 95
NICHOLAS, 74
NICHOLS, 3 4 5 13 65-67 83
NICHOLSON, 91 92
NICKELSON, 2 9
NICKOLS, 68
NIEUIMISTER, 56
NIX, 52
NOBLE, 51 52 58
NOELS, 52 60
NORMAN, 90-92
NORRIS, 6
NORWOOD, 19 23
NOX, 59
NUCKOLS, 87
OATSWALL, 85 87
ODELL, 53 55
ODLE, 84 85
ODOM, 35
OGLESBY, 37 38 40
OLIVER, 72 74 82 83
ORGAN, 15-17
ORKINS, 1
ORR, 2-5 10-12
ORTRIE, 72
OSBURN, 88
OSKINS, 8
OSTEN, 47
OSTIN, 47
OSTON, 44 47
OVERBY, 32
OWEN, 32 33
OWENS, 15-17
PAGE, 71 73-75 77 88
PAINIS, 69
PAREN, 15
PARK, 41
PARKER, 20 92
PARKS, 65 67-69
PARRET, 43
PARSELY, 23
PARTAIN, 98
PARTEN, 97
PARTON, 94
PASCHAL, 60

PATRIC, 15
PATRIE, 41
PATTERSON, 31 39
PATTON, 21 89
PAUL, 6
PAYNE, 24-27 29
PEACOCK, 50 51 58
PEEK, 99
PENDERGRASS, 16
PEPER, 88
PERMENTER, 22 23
PERVIS, 95
PETTIGREW, 23
PETTY, 86 95 97 98
PHARRIS, 71 74 75
PHILIIPS, 43
PHILLIPS, 20-23 43 77
PICKETT, 52 60
PIERCE, 22
PILKENTON, 40
PILKERTON, 32
PILKINGTON, 33
PILKINTON, 41
PIPER, 87 88 89
PITISON, 83
PITMAN, 17
PITTMAN, 17 19 20 22 23
PLASTERS, 53
POE, 92 93 95 98
POERS, 101
POLLETT, 20
POLSON, 23
POLSTON, 35
POOL, 24-26 32
POSTER, 42
POTETE, 15
POTTER, 92
POTTERFIELD, 24-27 29-31
POWELL, 81
POWERS, 1 3-7 10 11 13 87 101
PRATHER, 60
PRATT, 60
PRESNELL, 92
PRICE, 92 93 95
PRINCE, 84
PRIOR, 17 18
PRITCHARD, 82
PROSSER, 7
PRYOR, 94 96
PUCKET, 99
PULLIN, 36
PYATT, 91
PZEATT, 20
QUALES, 14
QUARRELS, 6
QUICK, 65 68
QUIGG, 64
RAGAN, 15
RAGLAND, 6 11 72 74

RAIS, 34
RALEIGH, 60
RAMSEY, 33 35 44-47
RANCH, 22 23
RAVENSCRAFT, 30
RAVENSCROFT, 25
READ, 65 69
READPATH, 65
REAVIS, 93
REDDEN, 82
REDFORD, 12
REDPOLK, 65
REED, 15 19-21 23 66-68 92
REEDE, 33 34
REEVES, 49-51 53 56 57
REEVIS, 54
REID, 10
RENFRO, 68
REYNOLDS, 65 71 92
RHODES, 25 50 51 53 54 57 58
RICE, 1 8 9 19 23
RICHARD, 16
RICHARDS, 17 36
RICHARDSON, 16 93-95
RICHESON, 28
RICHEY, 65
RICHIE, 83
RIDDLE, 68
RIEHL, 6
RILEY, 35 92
RING, 91
RIPPETOE, 76
RISH, 21
ROACH, 24 29 49 50 61
ROBBINS, 14-16 92
ROBERSON, 84 85
ROBERTS, 6 15 16 38 69 90 92
ROBERTSON, 35 36 91
ROBINS, 8 15 17
ROBINSON, 57 59
ROBISON, 85 86
ROBUCK, 34
ROCH, 65
ROGERS, 6 23
ROLAN, 96
ROLLANS, 19-23
RONDEL, 11
ROOK, 41
ROOKER, 16
ROOLEN, 91
ROSE, 92 97
ROSER, 2 10
ROSS, 55 56
ROUT, 32
ROUTT, 33
ROUTTE, 35
ROWLAND, 93-95
ROY, 4
RUBLE, 51 58

RUBY, 37-39
RUDDIE, 87
RUMMERFIELD, 55 58
RUNNER, 2 10
RUSSELL, 1 5-7 81
RUTHASSON, 16
RUTTE, 34
SADLAR, 76
SADLER, 70-72 74 75
SAINES, 58
SALDER, 71
SALE, 90
SALMON, 6
SANDERS, 85 87
SANDFORD, 71
SAWYERS, 23
SCARBROUGH, 91
SCHAEFFER, 60 64
SCHALL, 61 64 65
SCHMIDT, 64 65
SCOTT, 3 13 21 89 98 99
SCRIBNER, 99
SELLAR, 72
SELLARS, 74 75
SELLS, 16
SEMSON, 1
SHANDY, 51 52 59
SHANK, 64
SHANKS, 87-89
SHARP, 1 4-6 8 32 89
SHARPE, 32
SHAW, 28 33-35
SHEAFFER, 21 23
SHEALS, 64
SHEARON, 100
SHELBY, 20
SHELTON, 15-17 61 92
SHEPARD, 16
SHEPHARD, 16
SHEPHERD, 15 16 75 76
SHERON, 34
SHIFLETT, 34 35
SHILFETT, 34
SHINT, 90
SHIRLEY, 72
SHOCKEY, 92
SHOFER, 19 20
SHOFTNER, 19 21 23
SHRETE, 89
SHREVE, 88 90 92-94
SHRIEVES, 89 95
SHRIEVEY, 95
SHRITE, 90
SIGNIST, 87 89
SIGRIST, 90
SIMMONS, 65 66 87 89
SIMPKINS, 24 29
SIMPSON, 8 19 23 70 72-74
SINCLAIR, 97 98

112

SINGLETON, 16
SIRENS, 96
SITKEN, 59
SLADE, 87-89
SLANKARD, 19
SLAVENS, 67
SLIGA, 57
SLIGER, 51 54 58 59
SMALL, 64
SMILEY, 1
SMITH, 1-3 6-9 11 12 14-19 21
 23 25 30 31 37 40-44 46-48
 50 54 58 59 64-70 72 73 76-
 79 91 93 95 98-100
SMITHNOLD, 14
SMOTHERS, 32
SNIDER, 67 68 93-95
SNODGRASS, 3 6 13
SNOWDEN, 90
SNYDER, 68
SOFTNER, 23
SOLOMON, 54 56
SOUT, 42
SOWER, 23
SPARKSMAN, 17
SPECK, 46
SPEER, 80
SPENCE, 85 86
STAFFORD, 98
STAILEY, 90 91
STALEY, 90
STALLINGS, 73
STANTON, 71
STAPLES, 20
STARNS, 53 54
STATEN, 92
STEPHEN, 29
STEPHENS, 15 24-31 51 58
STERITT, 58
STERRITT, 51
STEVENISON, 95
STEVENSON, 22 23
STEWARD, 23
STEWART, 14 15 17 39 56
STIFLE, 51 58
STOCKTON, 79
STOKES, 35
STONE, 6 7
STORY, 93 94 97 98
STOUT, 42-48 91
STREET, 60
STRICKLAN, 67
STRUBBE, 64
SUMMERS, 88 90
SUPEONA, 68
SURFACE, 18
SURVANCE, 64
SUTTON, 83
SYNDER, 98

TACKET, 93
TACKETT, 94 96
TACLET, 93
TALLY, 16
TANNER, 55
TARTER, 93
TATE, 13 16
TAYLOR, 14 26 54 58 60 83 84
 91
TEE, 46
TEMPLETON, 17
TERRELL, 18
TERRY, 101
TETHRO, 87 90
THARNTON, 84
THOMAS, 1 4 6 18 26 29 35 84
 85 87
THOMPSON, 8 23 60 75 76 90
THOMSON, 83
THORNHILL, 51 58
THORNTON, 85 86
THORTON, 84
THRASHER, 6
THRESHER, 1
TILERY, 91
TILLY, 22 23
TILMAN, 3 10-12
TIMMONS, 25 29
TINCH, 44 48
TINGLE, 8
TINGLER, 8
TINLEY, 29
TINNING, 60
TIPPETT, 85 86
TIRRELL, 69
TITTLE, 72-75
TOLBERT, 73
TOLLETT, 23
TOTTEN, 20
TOTTON, 22 23
TOWLES, 35
TOWNSEND, 6 60
TOWNSLER, 6
TRADWAY, 19 61
TRAVIS, 39 101
TREDWAY, 61
TREMARY, 68
TRENARY, 67-69
TRENAY, 65
TRESSINRITER, 12
TRIGG, 96
TRIMBLE, 53 55
TRISSEMITER, 3
TROTTER, 80
TROUSDALE, 70 73-76
TUCKER, 83 95
TUGGLE, 33
TULEY, 24 25 29-31
TUMBLESON, 90

TURK, 6
TURNBOW, 93 94 96
TURNER, 6 31 35 50 57 90
TURNSBORO, 93
TUTTLE, 4 6 8
TUTTLER, 6
TYLER, 96
TYLEY, 26
UNICORE, 53
UPTON, 27
UZZELL, 41
VANDERPOOL, 54
VANDERSLICE, 50 55 56 58-60
VANNALA, 60
VANTREASE, 72 74 75
VAUGH, 33
VAUGHAN, 42 80
VAUGHN, 17 34 43 45 46 48 98 100
VINSON, 76 78
WADE, 1 3 4 6 11-13 22 23
WADSWORTH, 24-31
WAGGONER, 83
WAGONER, 82 83
WALDRIDGE, 3 13
WALKER, 17-19 26-28 33-35 46 55 82 83 95
WALLACE, 6 21 22
WALLIS, 15 22
WALLS, 6 33
WALTERS, 95 96
WANTLAND, 6
WARFIELD, 51 54 58
WARREN, 27
WASBURN, 20
WASH, 6
WATERS, 87
WATKINS, 2 3 5 7 8 10-12 39 93-96
WATS, 33 34
WATSON, 40-42 83
WATTS, 33 52 54 70-72 74-79
WAYMAN, 88
WEBB, 3 6 11 76 93
WEBSTER, 6
WEEKS, 6 32
WEEMS, 20
WELCH, 32
WESSON, 85 86
WEST, 22 60 91 92
WESVER, 36
WGONER, 84
WHEAT, 84 85
WHEELER, 94 96
WHIDBEE, 6
WHITAKER, 7 100
WHITE, 15 16 33 34 53 68 99 100
WHITEMAN, 3 13

WHITENACK, 1
WHITESIDES, 4
WHITMACK, 8
WHITSETT, 1 4 5 8
WHITSIDE, 2
WHITSIDES, 11 13
WHITTAKER, 2 10
WHITWORTH, 4 7 11
WI-----, 69
WICKHAM, 3 12
WILCOXEN, 26-28
WILKENSON, 92
WILKERSON, 80 81 92
WILKINS, 91
WILKINSON, 92
WILLAIMSON, 6
WILLIAM, 19
WILLIAMS, 6 17-19 23 27 28 53 66 90-93
WILLIAMSON, 4 6 69 70 72-79
WILLIS, 29
WILLOBY, 87
WILLON, 58
WILLOUGHBY, 90
WILLSON, 69 84 86
WILOUGHBY, 87
WILSON, 6 20 32 65 69 84 85 90
WINEHOLFE, 9
WINEHOPE, 1
WINKLE, 50 51 58
WINNINGHAM, 16
WINTON, 17
WISEMAN, 1 6 7
WITHERPSOON, 68
WITHERSPOON, 65-69
WOLF, 1 5 8 10
WOLFF, 2 3 6 8 9 11-13
WOOD, 17-19 50 51 90 91
WOODARD, 90
WOODS, 59
WOODSWORTH, 25
WOODWARD, 90
WOOLF, 3 13
WOOLFF, 5
WOOLFOLK, 6
WOOTEN, 97
WORKMAN, 50 57
WORLEY, 14-17
WORTON, 94
WRIGHT, 6 12 14 68
WRITE, 68
YARNELL, 90
YATES, 33 61
YORK, 52 56 59 90-92
YOUNG, 23 57 59
ZARNES, 4 9
ZORK, 57

Heritage Books by Sherida K. Eddlemon:

Missouri Genealogical Records and Abstracts:
Volume 1: 1766-1839
Volume 2: 1752-1839
Volume 3: 1787-1839
Volume 4: 1741-1839
Volume 5: 1755-1839
Volume 6: 1621-1839
Volume 7: 1535-1839

Missouri Genealogical Gleanings 1840 and Beyond, Volumes 1-9

1890 Genealogical Census Reconstruction: Mississippi, Volumes 1 and 2

1890 Genealogical Census Reconstruction: Missouri, Volumes 1-3

1890 Genealogical Census Reconstruction: Ohio, Volume 1
(with Patricia P. Nelson)

1890 Genealogical Census Reconstruction: Tennessee, Volume 1

A Genealogical Collection of Kentucky Birth and Death Records

Callaway County, Missouri Marriage Records: 1821 to 1871

Cumberland Presbyterian Church, Volume One: 1836 and Beyond

Dickson County, Tennessee Marriage Records, 1817-1879

Genealogical Abstracts from Missouri Church Records and
Other Religious Sources, Volume 1

Genealogical Abstracts from Tennessee Newspapers, 1791-1808

Genealogical Abstracts from Tennessee Newspapers, 1803-1812

Genealogical Abstracts from Tennessee Newspapers, 1821-1828

Tennessee Genealogical Records and Abstracts, Volume 1: 1787-1839

Genealogical Gleanings from New York Fraternal Organizations
Volumes 1 and 2

Index to the Arkansas General Land Office, 1820-1907
Volumes 1-10

Kentucky Genealogical Records and Abstracts, Volume 1: 1781-1839

Kentucky Genealogical Records and Abstracts, Volume 2: 1796-1839

Lewis County, Missouri Index to Circuit Court Records, Volume 1, 1833-1841

Missouri Birth and Death Records, Volumes 1-4

Morgan County, Missouri Marriage Records, 1833-1893

Our Ancestors of Albany County, New York, Volumes 1 and 2

Our Ancestors of Cuyahoga County, Ohio, Volume 1
(with Patricia P. Nelson)

Ralls County, Missouri Settlement Records, 1832-1853

Records of Randolph County, Missouri, 1833-1964

Ten Thousand Missouri Taxpayers

The "Show-Me" Guide to Missouri: Sources for Genealogical and Historical Research

CD: *Dickson County, Tennessee Marriage Records, 1817-1879*

CD: *Index to the Arkansas General Land Office, 1820-1907 Volumes 1-10*

CD: *Missouri, Volume 3*

CD: *Tennessee Genealogical Records*

CD: *Tennessee Genealogical Records, Volumes 1-3*